100 WAYS TO
LOVE
YOURSELF

100 WAYS TO
LOVE
YOURSELF
Inside and Out

WRITTEN BY TAURA STINSON

EDITED BY ASHLEY JOHNS

BELIEVE
BECOME
repeat

Published by Believe-Become-Repeat, Inc
Cover art by Sabina Kencana (Pages 14, 16, 22, 36, 39, 50, 51, 97, 120, 169)
Graphic Arts & Cover Typist by Muhammad Umair
Interior Typist – Richell Balansag
Page 93 Artist – Jane Goren
ISBN: 978-0-578-46167-0

The things that I believe
will become my reality today,
and for the days to come.
It's a perpetual cycle
of believing, receiving,
and becoming.
Believe. Become. Repeat.

#BELIEVEBECOMEREPEAT #100WAYSTOLOVEYOURSELF

CONTENTS

This book is dedicated to
the great loves of my life, my Mom ...
Yvonne Stinson, and my Dad, Willie Stinson.

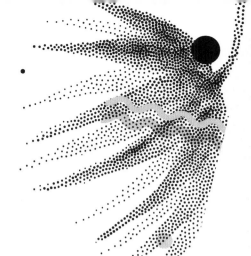

FIRST OF ALL,

I am a sacred place.

That doesn't quite roll off the tongue, but it's true and the moment I realized that, I began the process of genuinely loving myself. But don't be fooled; it is an ongoing practice I am always engaged in, even as I am writing this. I have been broken and am still picking up the pieces, yet I remain a sacred place; a space where I am gentle with myself and attentive to my own needs. No longer am I a punching bag for some boy trapped in a man's body to beat the life out of me and then spit his empty seeds into my ripe eager womb. That was back when I was wallowing in my brokenness with shards of myself sprawled about a darkened hollow room, where every time I dared to break free of the chaos, I'd trip over the remnants of my past.

I have since cleaned house.

Starting with the top floor, I planted seeds in my mind that would flourish in and around me. I then challenged the main feeling that haunted me to a battle: Scared. At that time, I was always fearful; jumping out my own skin and worried that I would never get out of that dark place. I felt trapped in a horror movie where the monster was always on my heels as I waded through pools of my own tears. I was tired and ready to face that monster and was appropriately scared when I realized the monster was me.

It was then that I decided to write the "longest email ever" (in her own words) to Oprah Winfrey, and "out of 131k in her inbox" (also in her own words) she responded to me with an email just as long. I spoke about this in greater detail in my first book; however, it was that revelatory moment that implored me to face the mirror. God knew the shelter I needed because I was spiritually homeless and in a relationship with someone who was legitimately trying his best to stop me from breathing. In those terrifying moments in that scary haunted house that was my body, mind, and soul, I was willing myself to become breathless as well. So yes, God knew that I either needed Prince to sing me a song in my living room or Oprah Winfrey to speak to me directly for me to wipe the fear from the window and see that there was a way out.

The next day wasn't magic or anything. I was still me, and there was still so much more work to be done, but for the first time in God knows how long, I had hope. I finally started to believe the tattoo that I had gotten on my arm earlier that year. It reads, "Believe. Become," and was also the subject line in my email to Oprah. That phrase came to me when a friend of a friend said, "Think. Say. Be" to me as the most beautiful gift of words at my birthday party. I ended up getting that tattooed on my neck, but I still wanted my own mantra—something grown from the seeds of my spirit. Then I came across a quote from the Buddha: "You become what you think."[1] Not only did the truth in it floor me, but also how it parallels Proverbs 23:7, "As a man thinketh in his heart, so he is he."[2] I heard that in church too many times to count as a little church girl, but I finally understood it, and it resonated with urgency. From that, my personal creed, "Believe. Become," was born, and that email from Oprah gently nudged me into putting those words into action for me.

I feel that it was around that time when I first earned my toolbox. I packed up and moved out of the scary house and slowly into the sacred place that I am becoming every day. I started this introduction by saying that I am a sacred place and that is because God lives in me. I don't play with adages like, "the devil made me do it," or, "the demons in me" because I am the fruit of my beliefs, and good or bad, I know that I know that I know that I will surely become what I believe.

So, with all of that said, I must admit that I am not a self-love guru. I do not have all of the answers, but I am more than willing to share the things that have worked and are currently working for me as I continue on this never-ending journey of *hella* loving myself. I am still unlearning things and picking the dirt from the fibers of my being that no longer reflect who I am.

I urge you to pack your things and move out of the places and spaces that once held you captive and find your new place in the sun—the fixer-upper that will eventually become the dwelling of your dreams... If only you believe.

xo
Taura Stinson

"ALWAYS REMEMBER THAT
YOU ARE BEING PLANTED,
GROWING, OR BLOSSOMING.
"GROWING PAINS" ARE
ONLY TEMPORARY!
VISUALIZE WHERE YOU WANT
TO BE FROM WHERE YOU ARE,
AND IT WILL NOT
RETURN TO YOU VOID."

— *Taura Stinson*

#BELIEVEBECOMEREPEAT #100WAYSTOLOVEYOURSELF

ABOUT THIS BOOK

This is so much more than a book; it is a conversation starter, a journey, an instructional manual, a reference guide, a storyteller, a mantra maker, a dream catcher, and, most of all, an experience that _you_ control. There are things in this book that may not resonate with you just yet, but as the mamas and grandmamas would say, "everything in time." This offering is from my sacred place. Not from a place of judgment, ridicule, shame, or anything else that may have been picked up along the way. It's a soft landing in a hard world, and you can rest here anytime, but as always when you enter someone's home, there are rules.

Rule Number One instructs you to do the work, and I mean in both a literal and figurative sense. There are a few exercises in this book (with the first one being on the next page). If you are in agreement with these rules then you will do them all. Some may seem silly but as I said before, I don't have all of the answers but I will gladly share what I do know in hopes that you, too, will move into—or in some cases back into— your own sacred place.

Rule Number Two is a deep commitment because it takes years or, for some, a lifetime to unlearn some of the toxic behaviors that have been with us for as long as we've been here on earth, but the "mess" has to go. What I mean by your "mess" refers to speaking ill to and/or about others, including yourself. As well as judging others or doing physical, mental, or emotional harm to others, including yourself. An addendum to this rule asks you to go on a negativity fast until you have finished reading this book. For further clarification, that means refraining from engaging in gossip, destructive media (including and especially social media), arguing, self-deprecation, or harm to others. If you agree with that, initial here!_____

Rule Number Three is as simple as it sounds. Write in this book. Put an old school paper bag cover over it if you want. If God ever blesses us to make our paths cross and I get a chance to sign your book, I want to write around the mascara stained tear puddle, or the deep dark coffee ring between two pages. This book isn't meant to stay pretty. It is meant to be lived in. It's a reference guide for you to dive into now and years from now.

Rule Number Four might not be exactly what you think. While I would love for you to share this book with all of your friends and family, when I say "share," I mean in a family-style setting. If you were seated at my family table you couldn't hover over the mac & cheese by yourself. It's substantial and meant to be shared. That is the same way I feel about this book. Don't hover over it. Test out certain exercises on friends and family. Print out the affirmations and stick them wherever you please in an effort to spread the love.

Rule Number Five was a life-saver for me. Still is. Rule Number Two is useless without Number Five because you can clean up your mess all day, but if you don't know what to do, or in this case say, everything will just get messy again. To remedy that, I am constantly speaking life (audibly optimistic and positive) over others and myself. When I can't speak through the tears, I rely on the sticky notes plastered throughout my apartment. And if those are not enough, I get into my car where a podcast is already synced to my Bluetooth and ready to fuel my spirit so that I am prepared for the day's journey.

Truth be told, sometimes I get into my car and just want to hear something ignant' and so I listen to it. There is no commendation here. What makes me ME is that I am part prim and proper, southern belle due to my birthplace, and partly radical Oakland (specifically East Oakland), which comes with a certain affinity to ratchet west coast music. (Insert the Kanye shrug)…I am unapologetically Taura Stinson. Be unapologetically you.

Rule Number Six – This rule flips everything that we ever learned on its backs. Generally speaking, we turn the lights off when we leave a room and close the door on our way out— but not here in this sacred place! Keep your light on, always. Keep it on not only so that you can see, but so that you can be seen as well. Don't shrink or minimize yourself in this experience. Be ALL you. Not the filtered you. Not the future you, but the you that you are at this very moment. Stand in your fullest glory and watch the light expand. Now let's consider another "light" as not just a tool of illumination, but as a reference to the weight of the baggage we tend to carry. In one of Erykah Badu's lyrics, she reminds us to "pack light"[3] because we can't fly or expect to navigate the darkness clearly while attached to such heavy loads. YOU HAVE TO LET IT GO! Pack light as a luminary and pack light when it comes to all that you are carrying. You cannot do it all, and you cannot take it everywhere with you.

I get that it takes time to drop the weight (or the wait), but move toward that goal rather than away from it. It works wonders. As does leaving the door open! This is a biggie for me because I was raised in a church where they cast out demons and did exorcisms regularly, and being afraid was par for the course. That was their intention. The more afraid the congregation was, the more inclined we would be not to stay in our places and earn our ticket to heaven. Over time I learned that God is LOVE! And if fear is not of God, then boom… it has no place in doctrine. If I would have closed the door to the thought that there are different ways to view God, I would still live in fear of Him, or would have come resentful.

There are six rules for a reason. The first five rules on this list are meant to be shared; however, this last ONE is just for you. **No one else can turn your light off or on, nor can anyone open or close your door.** I am a firm believer that God opens and closes doors for our protection, but here on this planet, you are the only person that can stop or start your flow. We give too much reverence or authority to people who just shouldn't have it. Leaving your door open allows you to be open to infinite possibilities, but always remember that in this space only the invited may enter.

For your first assignment, all you need is a pen/pencil and a little honesty.

Who are you? On the next page, write down as many words as you can that represent who you are on the inside. Right now, you can just rattle off words. Sentences and statements will come later, but for now, the assignment is to write down as many words as you can that represent who you are on the inside. There is no "right" or "wrong" in this exercise. Just remember Rule #1!

_____

_____

_____

_____

_____

_____

_____

_____

_____

_____

_____

_____

_____

_____

_____

_____

_____

_____

_____

_____

#100WaysToLoveYourself   #BelieveBecomeRepeat

Now that you have archived a snapshot of who you are internally, it's time to picture yourself. Not your past or future optimal self, but the you that's reading these words at this very moment! On the next page, I want you to draw that image of yourself. If you are not an artist, that's okay, neither am I. You will have a few more opportunities to improve this image ...such is life. And again, there is no right or wrong. Just remember Rule #1.

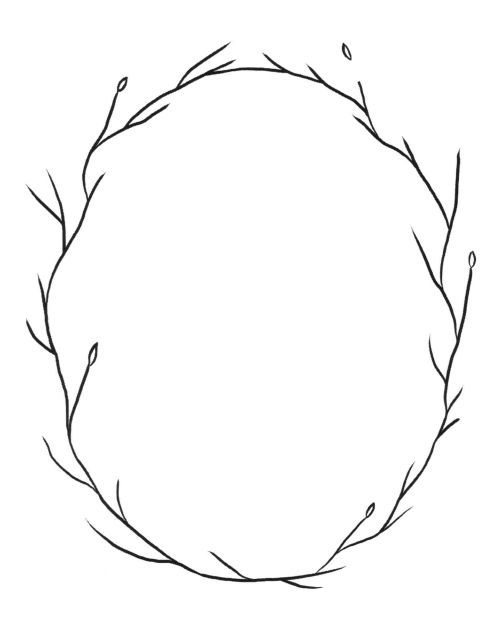

#BELIEVEBECOMEREPEAT #100WAYSTOLOVEYOURSELF

Remember that how you see yourself is important but not as important as your ability to wholeheartedly believe that you are making improvements from the inside out that will effectively enhance the above the image.

Now that we've set the tone, I should tell you a bit more about the book. *100 Ways to Love Yourself* is composed of 10 chapters featuring 10 extensive suggestions on how to love yourself better. Additionally, there are worksheets, affirmations and many of the tools needed to help you join the self-love revolution! It's truly the book I wish I would have had before I committed my forever to someone else. How could I have done that when I hadn't even begun to scrape the surface of self-love. That brings me to a point that I hear all of the time and totally disagree with. People say that we don't know ourselves in our 20s (some even say our 30s), and forget about it if you're in high school and college, but I disagree. The difference between me and an 18-year-old woman, who has no idea who she is or how to love herself, is information and education. Not a high school diploma or college degree, but what you have in your hand is one of many pieces of information designed to enlighten you. Let it. When I was 18, I graduated high school and didn't want to know anything about anything unless it was about music or my boyfriend. And guess what? I did extremely well with music because it was in alignment with my purpose, but not so much with the boys. Why? Because I didn't master the art of loving myself first. Instead, I was at the start of a very long and painful journey of pleasing others and dimming my light. As a result, I was bullied into marriage in my mid-twenties and stayed in it 12 years too long. I suffered through two extremely abusive relationships, prayer, meditation, weight loss, weight gain, suicide contemplation, self-hatred; and nothing helped me to see myself as the beautiful soul that I am until I learned to love myself.

The spark was set in me through freedom. I "liked' myself enough to finally leave my "home" with nothing but the things that could fit on the back of a small Toyota truck that belonged to my co-worker's husband. That spark would seemingly blow out when the storms continued to come, but this idea that I could become the best of my beliefs turned that spark into a fire that will burn forever.

I would have been receptive to this information years earlier, but my friend-circle's focus was not on self-love. I found myself in Atlanta, Georgia…so far away from my home in California. It was my college and grad school. I was thrust into misogyny and the objectification of women (if you remember music videos back then, then you know what I mean). That's why it's so important to know who your friends are. That's different from taking an inventory of your friends, which is also important, but I mean knowing who your friends *are*—their beliefs, thought processes and feelings. I was around people that were literally breaking me in two. My house had a revolving door on it for musicians to live and work, and while some were gracious, beautiful souls, others were bloodsucking vampires who would do anything to "make it," including sleep with the person I was in a relationship with…right under my nose. I was told that I was fat and ugly, and was called the "B-Word" more than I was called Taura, and that kind of negative reinforcement kept me from recognizing my own value.

It's my hope that you—yes you with this book in your hands— either love or learn to love your beautiful self. You don't have to go through the hell that I went through. Arm yourself with information and affirm your value daily and I am certain that it will change your life.

INTERIOR DESIGN

1. FORGIVE. I have nursed dead wounds back to life, just as I have carried pain that weighs a ton and I have paid for it dearly. You've heard the saying that anger is like drinking poison and expecting someone else to get sick? It doesn't work that way. You end up sickening yourself, period! According to Dr. Karen Swartz, director of the Mood Disorders Adult Consultation Clinic at Johns Hopkins Hospital, chronic anger increases the risks of changes in heart rate, blood pressure and immune response, and those changes increase the risk of depression, heart disease, and diabetes.[4] If we flip that on its back then we can discern that anger and disappointment rooted in unforgiveness has no place in our lives. It's easier said than done, but for your own sake, you have to try your hardest to let it go. You can't force anyone to tell you the truth, make amends, apologize, and you definitely can't make any changes to the past. When I realized that harboring anger and not forgiving people was likely the cause to some of the sickness in my own body, I let it go. I visualized myself walking to the trash and throwing it all away. Sometimes I'm like, *I thought I already took that trash out*, and during those times I just tie it up, throw it over my shoulder and throw it away again. The weightlessness of forgiveness feels better than resentment, anger, or bitterness ever could.

Learning to balance forgiveness is key because that's really what it's about. Forgiveness itself is an act of kindness, not only to the one who offended you, but to yourself as well. It frees up space in your heart and expands your thought capacity. Now when someone attempts to hurt you in the same way you will have a blueprint for that design. That's the good part about forgiveness. Of course, some of us will never learn and will continue to be broken in the same place…I did for a while until I refused to let my own brokenness be in vain. Now I turn forgiveness inside out and take actual notes on the lesson so that I am not allowing repeat offenders (or the same kind of offenders) into my sanctuary. I am a new student of the incredible Dr. Wayne Dyer. He was first introduced to me by someone who hurt me deeply so I wasn't receptive, but in this past year he hit me like a ton of light: At first, I squinted and had to shield my eyes, but now I am basking in his eternal sunshine. Although he has transitioned to another realm, his wisdom and teachings remain a viable resource for self-improvement and enlightenment. There was something I recently heard him say that became a part of me, so I added it to the quilt of life that is me. While chatting with Oprah on a Super Soul Conversation, Wayne quoted Mark Twain who said: "**Forgiveness is the fragrance that the violet sheds on the heel that has crushed it.**"[4] He then quoted an ancient Chinese proverb: "**If you pursue revenge, you better dig two graves.**"[5] The first quote reminded me of how very sweet forgiveness is, while the latter reinforced how weighted and toxic non-forgiveness can be.

2. HEAL. Some people only talk about healing but are not interested in doing the work to close the gaping wounds of yesterday…black and brown communities especially. My maternal grandfather was a strong man from Jefferson County Alabama. He was stern and, in my family, his word was the law. Even as a child I could sense his enormous presence. Instead of calling him Grand Daddy, Paw-Paw or Grandfather, we called him Big Daddy, and to my little self, he was as big as it got. He drove a pick-up truck and spat tobacco into a Folgers coffee can. He had big piercing eyes that could see right through all of us and instill the fear of God. I can still see him sitting there at the kitchen table playing cards with Uncle Jack and whoever else dared to battle him. Although he was unapproachable to most, he was like putty in my hands. He worked as lead security at the Birmingham Convention Center and I think that I might have been the only grandchild who was thoroughly excited about his celebrity run-ins backstage. Even as a young child, I always had this deep connection to music, so that was my way in with him, but not everyone was so lucky. Of course, he had special relationships with my other cousins and family members, and he softened as he grew older, but I still saw him as this big wall of a man that no one could ever climb, until recently.

I was in Atlanta for one day and got a chance to see several of my family members. We were backstage at a show that I sang background vocals for when my Aunt Faye pulled up a photograph of Big Daddy on her phone. It knocked the wind out of me. It was his eyes. They were deep and piercing, but not in the menacing, impenetrable way that I had remembered. They were filled with hurt.

The picture almost seemed to move. It was full of life, love, and something else that I didn't recognize as a child: pain. I don't know the source of that pain, but it was as clear as glass. The photo haunted me all the way to the tour bus. I crawled into my bunk and saw Big Daddy's eyes as soon as I closed my own. The pain was prominent and at that moment, I realized that he probably died with all of the pain rooted in unforgiveness, fear, hurt, guilt, and God knows what else.

I was too young to know how to recognize it then, but quite honestly it was like finding the source of pain within me, my mother, aunts, uncles, and cousins. I had long thought that my grandmother was the source of our hurt because you can only imagine how a guy named "Big Daddy" could wreak havoc on the heart of my grandma. When I was little, I often heard that she died from heartbreak. So naturally, I thought that some of the issues that plagued me and other women in my family stemmed from her pain.

This realization only cemented the fact that healing is important. If you don't heal, you bleed your toxicity on to the ones who you love and who love you in return. If you don't heal, you can become calloused and rough. If you don't heal, you are still broken, and broken people cut the ones who love them the deepest.

The thing about healing is that it comes in so many forms: obviously therapy, life coaching, classes, workshops, meditation, and prayer. And to the latter, I say this: God puts professionals in positions to help us to help ourselves. There are also people in and out of the church who have been blessed with the ability to help others on this spiritual journey. When most of us are hungry, we do not pray for food—we eat. If we are bleeding from a huge wound in our bodies, we see a doctor, but some of us leave it all up to prayer. I am not one of those people. Yes, I pray and yes, I believe that God still performs miracles and makes a way out of no way, but I also trust Him to lead me to people who can help soften my fall, strengthen my spirit, and nurture my soul. I am all about believing and becoming, but also learning. I am forever a student and the people that teach us are treasures. I am so grateful to them, for, without them and prayer, I would have spiritually poisoned myself to death years ago.

3. ALIGN. I grew up Pentecostal. They called my church non-denominational, but it was truly a Pentecostal experience on one hand. When I'd spend summers in Alabama, I'd go to church with my father's sister, Aunt Shug, who was Faith Apostolic one Sunday, and then attend my mom's brother's (Uncle Dandy) Church of Christ on the other Sunday. It was confusing, to say the least. I was, of course, always drawn to the music. My uncle, James McCurdy, who was the pastor of my church in Oakland (and later San Ramon) was incredibly talented. He sang with an internationally known Gospel quartet group called the Fantastic Viollanaires. He then went on to start his own group, The Gospel Clouds, but eventually heeded the call of being a pastor. I was a child at the time, so it was almost like being a pastor's kid.

To keep me from becoming another statistic in the "Say No to Drugs" era in Oakland, my mother made sure that I spent most of my free time in San Ramon with the McCurdy's or extended periods in Birmingham. Having all of these different types of spiritual input at such a young age was hard as a spiritually sensitive child. The fear of hell tormented me to the point of being unable to welcome or experience the beauty around and within me. This is a sensitive subject for me because I have literally gone through hell and high fire to get this point, and thank God for the growth and understanding, but I am still growing; still stretching and welcoming the hidden pockets of freedom that I discover in the dark places that used to bind me. My spiritual experience wasn't at all spiritual. It was primal. It was me against them in my mind. "Them" being demons, the devil, and dark forces, and because that was the focus of my fear, that's all that I would see. My parents even had to put double bolts on the front door because I ran out of the house as a small child, tormented by dreams. I would lay awake in bed pleading the blood of Jesus on so many nights that a huge part of my memories in elementary school included falling asleep in class. But you put out what you put in and all of the fear was pouring from me.

I have since learned to trust myself and the God in me, and that is also what you have to do for you. Getting to this point didn't come without out big conversations with God, endless tears, and to be candid, moments where I questioned everything, especially my beliefs. The biggest take-away has been that this is a personal journey between God and I, and I owe no one an explanation. You have to know for yourself and nurture your own beliefs. When you nurture a plant, you open the window and let the light in, water the soil and trim away the frayed, broken and dying parts. You have to do that spiritually as well, and the most important element for me is that the light that helps the plant to grow will never change. Yes, I had to cut off some things at the root, but the light perpetually remains. I call that light God. The God of the Universe and everyone in it and I am on a quest to mirror the image of this superior being in all that I do. When I was in those dark places, I was not in alignment. Imagine a train off its tracks; that was me, heading aimlessly in the wrong direction, but now I am back on track and know where I am going. Thank you, God.

Going to church, the synagogue, mosque, temple, or any other worship center doesn't necessarily mean that you are spiritually aligned with the Source. It's a personal relationship that requires commitment, respect, devotion, communication, and faith; all of which are shared between you and your maker. Not your pastor, priest, or other teachers. Obviously, I love worshipping alongside like-minded people, but sometimes I go it alone and that is okay. What's important to me and the progression of my spirit is to stay focused on the light. It is my feeling that when we are not aligned with the guiding light, we are aligned with darkness.

4. SLAY THE GREEN – EYED MONSTER. When I was growing up, my mother often told me how beautiful, smart, and talented I was, but even then, if I saw one of my classmates in some fresh new Guess jeans, I would stop at nothing until I also had a pair. It wasn't just with my classmates that I displayed this behavior, it was also Janet Jackson's "Pleasure Principle" music video. I wanted the black wig and the Guess outfit—I wanted to look just like Janet. My mom said no to the black wig, but she got the Guess jacket for me and I wore it until the stitches started to fall apart. I can only imagine growing up now, in a world where social media influencers and advertisement are king. Lately, I've noticed an influx of ads popping up on my phone. Ads that get me in my feelings like, *Wait…am I really that old? Why is this being suggested to me? And I know I'm heavy, but surgery? Is that what I need? Is that what she has? Will I feel better in that dress?* Those all are dangerous thoughts for any and everyone. As a result, I am weaning myself off of social media as a resource and rather hoping to be a beacon of light. That means less scrolling and more doing work to spread messages of self-love and cut the heads off of all the monsters that lurk there, such as jealousy and inadequacy. You will notice that I make several references to social media and its effects on how we view ourselves. The reason being is that I have personally encountered the negative impact that it has on women and girls. While supporting my book, *100 Things Every Black Girl Should Know*, I met countless girls and women at various panels, signings, and even via direct messaging, and a running theme has been how they feel inadequate when they compare their normal lives to the extravagant lives on Instagram, Facebook and Twitter. Not only that, but social media has also given bullying a platform like never before, and as a result, kids are taking their own lives and more and more, people are weighing their worth against altered images of filtered perfection. What I have to remember is that social media is like watching an endless stream of game highlights: they only show us the greatest plays (e.g., the flawless pass, or game-winning touchdown), while omitting far less glamorous moments (e.g., when someone breaks their leg, or the missed shot). It doesn't celebrate the full scope of the game—the pregame practice, teamwork, camaraderie or even the more "boring" rounds. Consider that the next time you are scrolling and feeling bad about yourself. I can only speak from my experience and, oh boy, am I guilty of comparing myself to those seemingly perfect people. I, too, have found myself being sucked into this vortex of dangerous thoughts and actions. I once purchased a fitness program, nutritional guide, lipstick and whatever else was being advertised to me, all in one day. When I stepped back to look at it I was embarrassed and needed to find the root to pull it out of me. I loathed certain followers and people that I followed, looking for a flaw in their "perfection" and when I'd find it, it made me feel better, temporarily. I have always been a supporter of my friends and family, but in those moments, I saw myself as my own enemy. I was constantly finding something wrong with everybody. I would say things to myself and my closest friends like, "Her edges are horrible," "her booty is fake," or, "her man isn't faithful." But that wasn't the real me talking, and that's hella not okay.

Rule Number Two is very important to remember here: CLEAN UP YOUR MESS!. I cleaned up my mess by spending less time online and more time on and with myself. These algorithms are so well programmed that they generate ads and suggestions that are tailored specifically for us. Our computers know us so well and ours triggers too. This is why radically loving yourself is so important. If you are on social media, realize that it's not a game. Take from it what you want, but remember that you don't NEED anything that is suspended in a virtual reality. God made all of us in an image that is reflective of His grace and mercy. Remember that next time you log in.

5. Be Free & Clear– I, like many of you truth seekers, love to study Rumi. Rumi is who I like to call the immortal poet because his teachings have and will continue to outlive him. Although he was an Islamic scholar and Sufi mystic (the inward dimension of Islam), his poems reach far beyond the barriers created by religion. I could go on and on about this 13th century poet, born Jalāl ad-Dīn Muhammad Balkh,[7] but instead I'll just stay on topic and bring one of his poems to your attention that was life changing for me:

> "Your task is not to seek for love, but merely
> to seek and find all the barriers within
> yourself that you have built against it."[8]

When I first read that poem I thought, "What barriers?" It wasn't until I tripped over a mountain of them that I realized how many I had created. The carnage left behind after the abuse created a barrier. My father's periodic absence in my childhood created a barrier. Then there were the hereditary barriers, and the silly barriers that I created when I was growing up, like reasons not to date a particular guy. But until you remove all those barriers they remain. I have always known that love knows no barriers, and that is a truth that I stand on, yet I had so many inside of me; thus, hindering my ability to even fully love myself. Believe me, it takes time and work to break them down, and part of my mission before you finish this book is for you to be at a place where you feel free and clear. You will know when the barriers are gone when you feel free to love, dream, and evolve. To seek love means that you are looking for the light, but in my experience, the light shines so much brighter and is more meaningful when you have faced the darkness. Although destroying those barriers may land you in some dark places, just remember the light is within you and when you remove the things that have been blocking it, you will be able to see everything more clearly.

6. KNOW NEW FRIENDS. Sorry Drake, but new friends are all right with me! That doesn't mean that old friends are bad, but we mustn't restrict ourselves from having new experiences with new people. If we're talking about self-love here, then this is essential because new friends can lift you in ways that some old friends cannot. Did you hear that? Let me say it again for the people in the back: **New friends will lift you in ways that some old friends cannot!** Your old friends know how you like your coffee, hate your relationship, or finish your sentences. But the new friend may introduce you to new coffee, ask questions that lead you to a deeper self and be the person that helps you to change the broken narrative.

The most important thing about your friendships is you! What kind of friend are you? Are you reliable, honest, forgiving? Once you know who you are and work on strengthening the positives, you will begin to attract like-minded people, and while you are on this journey of self-love, you may lose friends, and that's perfectly fine. I firmly believe that those who are meant to stay in your life will return and you all will laugh about it later, or they have made room for people who truly love and respect you. That said, on this journey of self-love, you will also gain friends, and it's a beautiful feeling. I have lost a few people in my life. People that I always thought would be there, but those blows were softened by the beautiful people that are now filling spaces I did not even know were empty. But don't worry about any of that. What's most important right now is for you to do your own self-work. Ask the hard questions and be honest with your answers.

So, the question that I have for you is this: what kind of friend are you? Be completely honest…it will only help your growth process. Circle the appropriate words below.

QUALITIES	DREAM PERSON	REALITY PERSON
Is he/she honest?	☐	☐
Is he/she reliable?	☐	☐
Is he/she secure?	☐	☐
Is he/she even tempered?	☐	☐
Is he she practical?	☐	☐
Is he/she a good listener?	☐	☐
Is this person consistent?	☐	☐
Is this person good with money?	☐	☐
Does this person live on his/her own?	☐	☐
Does he/she have sustainable employment?	☐	☐
Are you in agreement with core values/life goals?	☐	☐
Are you able to be yourself with this person?	☐	☐
Is this person malicious or violent?	☐	☐
Does this person hide important details?	☐	☐
Has this person cheated on you?	☐	☐
Does your intuition give you any alarms about this person?	☐	☐
Is this person an optimist?	☐	☐
Do you feel safe with this person?	☐	☐
Does this person make you a priority?	☐	☐
Does this person encourage you?	☐	☐
Do you balance one another?	☐	☐
Does this person love him/herself?	☐	☐

#100WaysToLoveYourself #BelieveBecomeRepeat

Remember your commitment to Rule Number One. This is hard work and only you can do it! It's not always pretty, but your fulfilled and empowered self requires this of you. Not for the 'gram or for your followers, but for you. The you that looks in the mirror through your eyes and into your soul, every day. She or he needs you to do this work, okay?

OKAY!

Now for some fun! Call two friends, new or old, mud or blood and ask them to give you two words to celebrate your friendship style and two words that could improve your friendship style. Write the answers below and use them to help you strengthen current and future friendships, and to repair those that have been broken along the way.

WHO DID YOU CALL?

WHAT ARE THE TWO WORDS USED
TO CELEBRATE YOUR FRIENDSHIP?

WHAT ARE THE TWO WORDS USED
TO DESCRIBE AREAS THAT YOU
NEED IMPROVEMENT ON?

DO YOU AGREE WITH BOTH?

IF SO, HOW DO YOU PLAN TO
IMPROVE ON THE AREAS OF IMPROVEMENT?

#BELIEVEBECOMEREPEAT #100WAYSTOLOVEYOURSELF

36

7. Clean House. Unlike Rule Number Two, when I say clean house, this time I am referring to your spirit house. One of my dearest friends is an organizer and before starting a project she has an assessment meeting with her client. This is probably the easiest part because it's quite idealistic. You just sit down and talk about the things that you will get rid of…the things that are broken, no longer serve you or just take up too much space. Then comes the actual purge. She goes in with a team and labels the things discussed into three categories: keep, giveaway or trash.

That's when things get challenging. Holding her manifest, Roxy separates the items and gets to work, but there are always things that clients refuse to let go of (e.g., broken glasses and electronics, moth-eaten and stained clothes, boxes of papers, towels with holes, etc.). Whatever the item, they can come up with an excuse to hold onto it. "Those clients," she says, "are the clients that either cancel appointments or waste money," by not allowing her to do her job. Her ideal clients make the list and do not check it twice. They trust her to do her job, follow her recommendations and they are always happier in the end. My goal is to be in that group.

I, like many of you, have so many things that I am holding onto that need to be in the trash pile, but I can't seem to let them go. So, I thought that it might be a good exercise for us to let go of some things together! But remember this: nobody can clean your soul for you but you. Counseling is awesome and church is divine, but you, and only you can clear your spiritual house of the things that no longer belong.

I have made a three columned list of things that I carry with me spiritually, emotionally, and mentally that I need to keep, giveaway or trash. I am keeping things like my ability to love hard, dream, and my faith. I am giving away lessons that I have already learned in hopes that someone doesn't have to go through what I did to get similar results. And I am trashing mediocrity, being overly emotional, and the way that I view my physical body. Consider the lessons and/

or resources you have acquired, whether from hardship or success, that have the potential to legitimately help someone else who may need it at some point. You drank the water, now share your bottle with someone else in hopes that they will refill it and offer someone else a drink. Share the steps with others that helped you to overcome your darkest or most challenging hours. If someone were to ask me about how I survived domestic violence, I could talk all day and provide resources that could potentially save lives. Additionally, I have resources for young songwriters that could help shape their futures. What is in your giveaway pile?

The trash pile will write itself. The top of my list was people-pleasing, non-reciprocal relationships, poor eating, etc.

Now it's time for you to write your own list. *P.S., I know that poor eating seems like a physical thing, and it may be, but when I found out my "why," I knew that it was rooted deeply within. Keep that in mind as you start, continue or re-approach this exercise.*

KEEP

GIVEAWAY

TRASH

#BELIEVEBECOMEREPEAT #100WAYSTOLOVEYOURSELF

8. Pack Light. Just in case you didn't "get it" in the rule section of the book, I thought to expound. I love me a good double entendre, and this one is one of the two's that I love best. If you haven't heard "Bag Lady" by Erykah Badu then I am not judging you—maybe your musical taste, but not you. My recommendation is to go listen to that song as soon as you put this book down! But in all seriousness, this woman said something that I often reference when life seems to weigh me down. The lyrics, "Bag lady, you gone' miss your bus./ You can't hurry up, cause you've got too much stuff,"[9] spoke to me and encouraged me to make some changes in my life. This song could have been about anyone, but it spoke directly to me. It tells a story of a young woman who carries the weight of the world on her shoulders and how that impedes her movement and causes her to miss out on her destiny. It was an accurate description of my life at that time. I was covered in pain from head to toe, both physically and emotionally. I couldn't listen to the song because I knew like hell that I needed to "let it go," but I felt I didn't have the tools I needed to do so. That's what I am hoping that this book is for someone: **The knife that cuts the cord of anything that does not serve you**!

But before you physically let go, you've got to clean house. I know it because I did it myself. You can't welcome love in if you don't have any room, so make space for it. Close your eyes and visualize a suitcase, or a trunk, or moving van if you need to. Now purge. Get rid of all of the things that do not bring out the best of you. Throw out all of the things that have hurt you. Remove the people— YES PEOPLE— who do not mean well for you. Once you do this successfully, you will start to make space for goodness, and you may have to do this forever. Just this morning, I checked my bag. Lying in bed before my feet hit the ground, I visualize my bag. I can see it like it's right in front of me: It resembles the trunk that my mom used to put my toys in; black with brass hardware, and weathered, but whole just like me. There are still a few things in there that have no business being there; still some things collecting dust, but it's lighter than it's ever been, and I am constantly working toward whittling this trunk down to a carry-on size backpack. Recently, after taking inventory of the contents within, I closed my trunk and could see the light spilling out of it. The light wasn't there before when there was no room for it amidst all of the negativity I was carrying with me. So "packing light" is important for two reasons:

1) To lessen the load so that you can move more freely and with clarity,
2) To be a beacon of hope—not just for everyone else, but primarily for yourself.

9. BE THE BEAUTY IN BROKENNESS. If you haven't been broken yet then wait for it, because it's coming. We are not smooth and flawless, filtered people in real life. It's the bumps, bruises, gaping holes, scratches and crutches holding us up that makes us beautifully flawed and whole beings. A part of that is being willing to show your scars, and that's so important because we have all learned to cover them so well, but there is power in them. Power for you and for others who are looking for a way off the same jagged path that you once walked along as well. Sometimes all we need is to see someone who withstood the fire for us to know that we can make it out alive, too. Keeping our stories hidden only empowers the oppressor, whoever—or whatever—that may be. Reclaim your power and shine through the darkness. Be willing to share your story when someone runs their finger against your scar and asks, "What happened here?" Be willing and eager to speak up about the things that used to bind you, from which you have broken or are currently breaking free (e.g., mental illness, abuse, terminal, or acute illnesses, etc.). Of course, most of our scars are invisible, like the ones one our egos, hearts and scattered throughout our past. Share your map with others in hopes that they won't have to jump through the same hoops of fire that you did. We gain nothing from hoarding wisdom and tools of navigation. Therefore, if you already know the way, why not illuminate a path for someone else?

Every time I see a flower breaking through concrete—usually wild and battered, but still beautiful—I acknowledge its beauty. From one living thing to another: **"You broke through concrete and your petals are still beautiful."** Let that be the metaphor you meditate on when you consider how far you have come in your personal journey.

10. Be Like Water! Doing my part to save the ocean from being filled with plastics. So every day I pour filtered water into a container. It's a forced moment of stillness. I can't rush it. No matter what I do, it takes its time and flows as it does, so I take that time to cement my intention for the day, or at least try to. Sometimes my thoughts wander, and I imagine them attached to a leash and I pull them closer to me so that they don't go too far, but this one thought became a way of life for me. As I watched the water rush in one morning, I noticed how loud it was in my container. You know how drops in a bucket sound? It was like that, but fast-paced and just super loud on this particular day. I was so annoyed, but as the water continued to fill the container, the sound grew quieter. It was still progressing, still being filled but it made less noise. As soon as it finished, I pulled out one of my yellow sticky notes and wrote "Be Like Water" on it and posted it on my fridge. It gets the most questions when guests are visiting, wading through the gallery of notes. My answer grows and grows because in the beginning the take-away was that the water was loud like waves breaking against the sand and quieted in the deep. I associated it with social media at the time. I was going through a period where I was annoyed with everyone's peacocking. I thought, *Is life really that perfect?* They were there posting fabulous vacations, tummy reducing teas and just the general "look at me, look at me," but nothing felt authentic. It was like the sound of the water beating against metal first thing in the morning. I wanted to be the water that was buoyant and deep, but I soon realized that loud annoying sound was a part of the process. A process that I had long since gone through. Yes, I have beaten my chest and flapped my wings, but now my water is deeper, calmer, and withstanding the tests of time, wave by enormous wave. Water washes us clean, nourishes us and keeps us alive. With that, I want to be a water friend. A water daughter. One day, a water mother. A water wife. It's a stretched analogy to some when I share it, until I say, **"Who wants dirty water?"** I strive to be a clean life source. A water friend to others and to myself. Someone who is as clear as glass with my intentions and who can withstand the cold and take the heat.

LANDSCAPING

1. SMILE. This might sound silly or cliché, but it's what I do in the mirror every single morning that I am gifted another day of presence. I am present and I am as kind to myself as I am to my family and friends. When I see a passerby, I don't look straight ahead or fix an awkward gaze on a random thing until my peripheral loses sight of the obligation to…

JUST

BE

KIND!

Instead, I smile at strangers and if they can get my best, so can I! If this sounds crazy to you, then you probably need to do it. I have a sticky note on my mirror that reads: "Smile 25 times today." It used to simply say "Smile today," so I am proud to add twenty-four more smiles per day. I am not sure if that number will grow, but right now 25 feels good!

I should clarify that the goal is to smile with your heart. Curling and stretching the edge of your lips might be what you have to do until it feels right, but again, that isn't the goal. The goal is to feel peace and happiness radiating from within. The smile is an added bonus. I was having the worst day and was just shopping around Marshall's when a woman smiled at me. I thought someone was behind me, but when I looked behind me and saw no one, she was still smiling. It warmed my heart. She didn't want anything but to shine a little sunshine on my sadness. I know she saw it because it followed me everywhere that day, and after our exchange I tried it myself, smiling at a woman who was seemingly as frustrated as I was, and I felt even better. She started a cycle of kindness that I continued to carry within me and share with everyone on my path. I now try and do this everywhere I go. **Smiling is an unspoken language that is universal and warms the heart.**

2. BE WHO YOU SAY YOU ARE. That should be a given but sadly it isn't. Even some of the biggest and brightest stars are guilty of pushing a narrative that they themselves are not walking in. I have been in rooms with women that give off so much shade that you would think clouds were in the room, especially in the entertainment industry. I have watched women stand up as advocates for female empowerment; diversity and inclusion for women in entertainment but their actions don't align when it counts.

And

It

Counts

All of the time!

Don't be the person that pours oil on the mountains after you reach the top and then stand there holding a banner of love while watching everyone else slide down with every stride. Be the love that you needed during your toughest times.

Be the yes that you needed when everyone said no, and be the warm soft landing for someone who can barely fathom taking another step.

I am on this journey of self-love, but again, I am not a self-love guru who has all of the answers. And if I chose to walk in anything less than love that would make this entire book a lie. I'm not perfect by any means. In fact, I can be socially awkward, fumble when I speak and have challenging days just like everyone else. Often times I myself have to return to the exercises in this book, but even so, I am still a sponge for love and light, and I stand in who I am. Wishing the same for you and your tribe!

3. SECURE YOUR OWN MASK. I was almost ready to start shouting and praising on a recent flight. What I learned is that **when you are ready for the message, the messenger will appear**. The other day, the messenger was a flight attendant standing a few feet ahead of me, demonstrating the safety features of the aircraft. We were mostly a captive audience since WIFI was not working on the tarmac, and for the first time in a long time, I listened attentively and was mind-blown at how perfectly one of the safety instructions could be applied to life: "Be sure to secure your own mask before assisting others." Although that may sound easy in theory, when applied to real-life situations, it can be hard as hell! For some of us, the idea of taking care of ourselves before we tend to other people's needs can seem counter-intuitive and selfish; however, it is crucial that we take time to address our own needs so that we can approach any situation with confidence, energy and clarity.

To put it in simple terms, I LOVE to cook, but hate to eat right after cooking. I'm sure this has something to do my senses being engaged throughout the process...so when I'm done I generally need a minute. I used to cook and then immediately serve fresh plates to my guests, but by the time I was ready to eat, I wouldn't have a chance to fully enjoy my own meal because it was all gone. These days when I cook, I make myself a plate first, write my name on it and store it, and *then* serve my guests. This has saved me from wondering if the Gumbo really was good, or if there was enough garlic on the bread. That's a simple way to explain this life rule, but until you are in practice of putting yourself first, it will seem like a foreign concept. It's also hard to put yourself first when the kids, spouse, parents, boss (or whomever else) always seem to require your immediate attention; but try to make the time! I started off with a simple list, and here's your chance to do the same. To give you an idea,

I just made an agreement to consider my dietary needs first. Because I am often cooking for the people I love and therefore considering everyone else's do's and don'ts, I am rarely paying enough attention to my own. As a result, **I am hella flexitarian** and it shows. One day I am following a low carb or keto diet, and the other I am just eating bar food, but if I were somebody else, like a loved one that I care for, I would treat me better. If I were someone else I would make my food first, put aside and then worry about everyone else's plate. I can remind my parents and loved ones to be healthy, get rest or even go out and have fun and not do the same for myself, but those days are over for me, and I hope that they are for you too.

After you make this list, don't forget to sign your name!

ways that I will put myself first!

_____

_____

_____

_____

_____

_____

_____

_____

_____

_____

_____

_____

_____

_____

_____

_____

_____

X_____

sign your name above

_____

#100WaysToLoveYourself   #BelieveBecomeRepeat

Great, now you have a contract with yourself. Honor it!

4. FIND YOUR FINE. I don't care who you are or where you are in your glow-up process, but I do hope that you like something about your outer self. Name three things right now, go!

THREE THINGS THAT I LOVE ABOUT MY EXTERNAL SELF

☐ _____

☐ _____

☐ _____

(SUBJECT TO CHANGE)

#BELIEVEBECOMEREPEAT #100WAYSTOLOVEYOURSELF

50

Now, I'll share mine…just in case those spaces above are still blank and you need an example.

THREE THINGS
THAT I LOVE
ABOUT MY
EXTERNAL SELF

☐ LASHES

☐ SKIN

☐ TEETH

(SUBJECT TO CHANGE)
#BELIEVEBECOMEREPEAT #100WAYSTOLOVEYOURSELF

To be honest, this would have been an impossible task for the past me's (yes, "me's", but more on that later)! When I was a kid, I used to take scissors and cut my eyelashes because some of the kids called me Llama Lashes. Oh, what a compliment it is now, but back then they laughed at me so hard that I literally cut them down to avoid the endless mockery. Obviously, that stopped nothing, because they found something else to bully me about…anyway…that's another story, so moving right along.

My second choice was my skin. I work extremely hard for this effortless fair-weathered glow. For starters, I drink mostly water…at least a gallon every day. I also buy every serum and face cream known to woman, and am proud of it! I have been able to provide facemasks for an entire group of women without even shopping. Seriously, we had a mask & mimosa party and I did two red carpet facials on two friends, and one for myself. I also had enough paper masks to go around several times… it's not a game.

Okay, so, the last external thing that I like about myself are my teeth. I don't gaze at them or give them too much thought, but a friend recently told me that I had nice teeth and I thought, "Mmph? Maybe so."

SIDEBAR: I chose "teeth" because I could not find something else that I love when I look in the mirror. I love my soul, my commitment to my people and all sorts of things that you cannot see, but finding physical attributes was tough. My teeth are just teeth, but I do have a good smile and they are white-ish. This was a confirmation of my reasons for loving myself. I am definitely the best person to write this book! I want to love the parts of me that I have always hated, but it's hard. I am not fat and happy, mmmkay? I want to be sexy and fine and make no apologies for my rock-hard abs peeking through my crop top. I want to say that I love my tummy or that I love my booty.

The truth is that they both need work. In theory, I need tons of work on loving what I see. I think most of us do. I should also mention that soon after I wrote this passage, I took a break from writing because I had a terrible reaction on my scalp and skin from hair dye. I was headed out of the country on tour and wanted to dye my edges before I left. It usually goes off without a hitch, but not this time. This time I was itching from head to toe and still had to go to Europe anyway. I couldn't find anything to help and was in sheer agony. My scalp was redder than I had ever seen, as was the skin on the side of my face, my ears, and my hairline. I was there for 13 days before being able to visit the doctor and seek advice from my friend Chantel who's an amazing alopecia and hair/scalp expert. To this day I have a bald patch on the side of my head. Fortunately, it's growing back, but the experience humbled me in a way that I didn't even know that I needed. It taught me so many lessons, the main one being that bald spot or not, I am still a growing, ever-evolving human being with flaws. So, after that experience, my three answers evolved to the following.

THREE THINGS THAT I LOVE ABOUT MY EXTERIOR SELF!

- **My eyes** – Because I can see this beautiful world, as well as the people I love and any dangers ahead…I am so thankful for my sight.
- **My ears** – Without my ears, I could not be who I am. Music shapes and moves me. I love that I can hear music and the sound of the wind. **I lov**e that one of my ear lobes has two lobes—evidence that my mother and I were fiercely connected when I was in utero. Her ear was split when someone pulled her earring too hard, and then I was born with a split in the same section. So technically, I have three lobes, and I like that I am unique in that way.
- **My belly scars** – I had exploratory surgery at 18 months old after being hit by a car. As a child, I wore bikinis because I had no idea some people may find my scars repulsive, but the older I got, the more self-conscious I became. Then I spent a lifetime afraid that someone would see them. I cov-

ered myself in Kaftans and ponchos so that no one would stand a chance, and it worked; however, the more I covered myself, the heavier I became, both emotionally and physically. One day I stood in the mirror fully naked and I faced the scars. I wanted to cry, and I was ready to cry, dammit. I had the Kleenex ready, but the scars spoke to me: "if it weren't for me, you would have never come to California. I was a part of your destiny." It was a divine revelation that I will never forget. I now thank my lucky scars instead of condemning them.

I also want to clarify that lashes, skin and teeth were perfectly fine answers, but I am on an excavation mission and digging as deeply as I can until I get the gold. We are all at different points in our journey and there are no right or wrong answers.

BUT!!!!

If you do have lucky scars, honor them! And for further clarification, lucky scars are people and things that hurt you but actually turned out to be a blessing or a catalyst for one.

5. GIVE TIME TIME. If paper cuts hurt like hell, imagine the time it takes for the massive breaks in our hearts to heal. There are no band-aids for that. No quick fixes or CliffsNotes. **You simply have to go through it in order to get to the other side.** When you rush and weave through the road to "get there" you are more likely to crash into the same wall that debilitated you in the first place. Stay in the slow lane, drive on the shoulder, or take baby steps if you need to…just stay on your feet with your intentions fixed on your healing and no one or nothing else except God. It won't happen overnight, but if you keep inching forward in the right direction, you will reach your destiny and you won't be late because it has already allotted us the time that some of us relentlessly stress over.

6. **LOSE WAIT.** This is a recycled *Call to Action* from my last book, *100 things Every Black Girl Should Know*. It's not a typo because I am certainly in no position to tell anyone to "lose weight," but what I know for sure is that procrastination is the enemy of progress. If you want anything to change in your mind, body or spirit, waiting is not an option. Sure, there are instances where we plant the seed and wait for the harvest, but we are the harvest! So when the harvest comes, we water it, give it sun, and nourish it or else it will die. The same goes for your dreams. They will wilt and lose their potency the longer that you steep it in crippling doubt. Don't let your soil dry up, work on it now! If you are reading this, then the good thing is that you are here. You are a living, breathing human being who might even be a serial procrastinator (and I can only call you out on that because I have been one myself). The waking period for me was finally leaving an abusive relationship, but it still took tons of work and deep dark pitfalls to get myself to where I am now. Losing wait is something that we have to do both internally and externally for ourselves. I know that you have heard the old adage: "Don't put off till tomorrow what you can do today." And that's just it. Self-Sunday is a thing in my household. We do facials, wash and deep condition the hair, and although this might sound corny, if I am slacking anywhere in my progress, I stand in front of the mirror and reaffirm my confidence. It is a practice I highly recommend. There is an entire section on affirmations, and if you are stuck or doubting yourself in anyway, I highly recommend jumping to the "Affirm" chapter and start reciting them now! Before you turn to the page, remember Rule Number One, **"Do the Work!"**

Very rarely do people just read a book to fix themselves. That's why I designed these sections that allow you to personalize this experience, but don't stop there, in fact DON'T STOP. Keep it moving! Keep flowing! Keep it going and work on knowing the difference between rest and complacency. We all need rest, (I'll talk more about this in the next *Call to Action*), but some of us use that as an excuse to wait. We wait for a savior, a sign, or a knight in shining armor, but you have everything you need to get to the next level inside of you, period. Luke 17:20-21 says that "the Kingdom of God is within you!" So **stand strong knowing that your squad is royal and well equipped to face anything in front of you!**

SIDEBAR: I am in my late forties and cannot stand that my weight still has a hold of me. Most of you don't know me from a hole in a wall, but those of you who do know that my weight has been an issue since it wasn't even an issue. What I mean by that is I wish that I were currently as fat as I thought I was when I was in my girl-group. Back then my weight fluctuated between 145 and 150 lbs., and I thought I was totally fine until someone from our label told me that I should watch my weight, so I did. I started to obsess over it, giving it power that it never before had over me, and then boom—I really started to pick up weight. Then I lost it following the disbandment, and that was one of the most confident times in my life. I was happy behind the scenes writing songs and living my young, golden life. But then I got married... That's when I started to believe that I was every bit of the "fat-bitch" my ex called me almost daily. It was like soul junk food that he fed me daily and I ate it up, and with every word, I became what he wanted me to believe I was. I am sharing this with you in hopes that it will help you to lose wait. Not weight, but the *wait* that keeps you from expressing your best self now: procrastination. Kick that enemy of progress, success, and access out of your wheelhouse once and for all! I used my weight as an example, but that was not the only thing that was unhealthy about me. It was my mindset and my self-confidence, self-respect, self-worth and, of course, self-love! All of me needed healing, and that's why I am writing this book, because I wish that back then I had a book that spoke directly to me from someone easy to understand and relate to, like a friend, sister or the highly attentive and wise stranger at a bar! That's what I hope this book becomes for you. I hope that you really commit to doing the work, and not stopping when you reach the final page. If you want it, get it now. **Don't wait, don't cheat yourself...just do it now. You'll thank yourself later.**

7. **REST. RECHARGE. REPEAT.** The irony in this moment is that I am writing this segment in between the wick of a candle burning on both ends. I am in the process of moving. Only the next city over, but you would think I was moving cross-country. Everything is everywhere and I am feeling more than overwhelmed, so before I head out to a friend's birthday party, I thought to check in with all of you self-lovers. I spoke to a friend who heard my voice, all stressed and groggy who asked, "Why are you going out if you're so tired?" And just as I was about to throw in the towel and stay home, I decided to do what's best for me. I don't owe anyone an explanation, but I do want to shed some light on this thought process. Resting, for me, usually includes my feet kicked up with a book, listening to a podcast or my binge watching my favorite TV show. Google's definition of rest is to "*cease work or movement in order to relax, refresh oneself, or recover strength.*" That could include sleep. In fact, a part of my rest ritual is to turn off my phone and alarm before sleeping. I usually wake up fairly early with the help of my alarm, but not when I am in rest mode. To recharge, regardless of the official definition, is relative. It's personal and unapologetically your process. Sometimes I recharge with sleep too, but because I spend so much time alone or with a close group of people, my idea of recharging is getting out the house. Tonight, it's a friend's birthday party, but sometimes it's the beach, dinner, a museum, sip & paint, or whatever else deepens or widens the connection part of this human experience. I was about the type that "working out" is how I recharge, but I can't lie to y'all! I want it to be and it's on my bucket list,…but I'm not there yet. Pray for a sistah! Although I'm very serious about that, but I'm not beating myself up over it. I have made tremendous progress! I used to have severe insomnia, taking sleep meds just to get a few hours of sleep, but I have learned to reclaim my peace, and now I schedule it. Remember that I mentioned Self-Care Sunday? Yes, I am mostly booked on that day and the person I meet with is myself. That doesn't mean that I don't sometimes go on dates or hang with friends at some point on that day, but I do carve out me time.

The key to resting, and recharging is simple: do what feels good to you, and then repeat. Rest your eyes if you are in front of a computer all day, or rest your feet if you are always on them. This sounds like it should be common knowledge, but it isn't. Unfortunately, some people just go and go until there's nothing left. This new (self-lovery) journey that you are embarking on requires you to bring your whole self, and you can't do that if you have worried or worked yourself half to death. Below are a few ideas to help you to get your R's on.

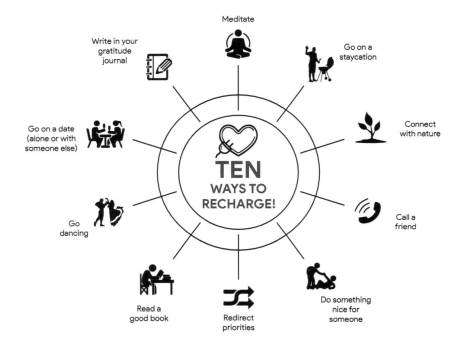

Meditate

Write in your gratitude journal

Go on a staycation

Go on a date (alone or with someone else)

Connect with nature

TEN
WAYS TO
RECHARGE!

Go dancing

Call a friend

Read a good book

Redirect priorities

Do something nice for someone

#100WaysToLoveYourself #BelieveBecomeRepeat

8. **FIND YOUR VILLAGE.** I am certainly preaching to the choir, people. I can isolate myself like the best of them. I will retreat to my apartment and talk to almost no one, but that is not how we were designed to be. We are a communal people, and "me" time is definitely a thing, but that is only a part of the big picture. News flash. **The big picture is not a selfie! Your village includes you, your**

loved ones, and the people who you can learn from and teach. Finding your community does not have anything to do with your geographical position, especially since you can go anywhere in your mind. And your real community stretches far beyond the confines of neighborhoods and zip codes. Just don't take all of this on by yourself! House Rule Number 6 is important to consider here because leaving the door open and the lights on are essential! While you are community shopping be sure to only consider those who are in alignment with your values and goals, and who challenge and call you on your BS. Leaving your door open creates an endless flow of give and take. Closing the door and turning off your light serves no one here, especially not you. Be all in and see how life-changing it can be. When I joined the Academy of Motion Pictures Arts & Sciences, I found a wonderful community of free-thinkers in this beautiful sub-community of creatives, and I love being a part of it! My best friend's mom, Auntie Louise, is a part of GirlTrek, a walking community that keeps her active and among like-minded women who have similar goals. Your people are out there, you just have to go and find them, or keep your light on so that they can find you!

Okay, now it's time to do the work. Take a moment to consider the individuals within your community, and in the space below, I want you to write their names under the category you believe they most accurately fall under. Now, keep in mind that some or all of those are interchangeable, so be sure to include them twice in the spaces provided below should that be the case.

L♡VED ONES	TEA🍎HER	🎓STUDENT
_____	_____	_____
_____	_____	_____
_____	_____	_____
_____	_____	_____
_____	_____	_____
_____	_____	_____
_____	_____	_____
_____	_____	_____

#100WaysToLoveYourself #BelieveBecomeRepeat

The point of this exercise is for you to identify your tribe and their roles in your life. If there is any doubt or confusion, always refer back to this list.

9. **BE THE LOVE THE WORLD NEEDS.** I know it's hard sometimes, but that is honestly what we are here for: to cycle love. If you picture it like a ball of energy that we pass to one another with our smiles to passersby, kindness to strangers and loved ones, and good intentions to and for all, then you know how important this cycle is. Sadly, humanity has been the antithesis of that ball of beautiful, merciful, and glorious light. In my lifetime, I have never witnessed hatred as blatant as it is now, and today after watching yet another heartbreaking newscast, I wondered **what if we all believed that we could change the world?**

10. **LIKE YOURSELF.** These days everyone talks about "securing the bag." Well honey, "liking yourself" is the **REAL** bag! But be forewarned, it is a lot easier said than done. We are hyper-critical when it comes to our standards for others, but I encourage you to put yourself under that same microscope and see what you find. **YOU ATTRACT WHO YOU ARE**, so if you are looking around pointing out the things that you dislike in your friends, then it is highly probable that you have some of those exact same characteristics yourself. **The beauty is that you are the author of your own book and the thumb to your remote control, so you can CHANGE IT at any time!** In my opinion, the key to change is acknowledgment. It took me a long time to like myself but once I acknowledged some of the things that I did not like, it enabled me to render them powerless. It doesn't happen overnight, but with dedication and consistency, you can learn to truly like the essence of who you are.

Another thing that I found helpful was to write down a few attributes in others that I really like. Below you're going to write down five things that you do not like about yourself along with five things that do you like about someone you know. Remember we all are flawless through the lens of a filter, so this is not the place where you write about your favorite celebs. This exercise is a little tougher than it seems because you can't possess the things that you like about someone else. They should be goals. Like my mom, she approaches everything gently. I don't have that. She is also a great listener, but sometimes my ADD. won't let me be that great…You see what I mean? Write about the attributes of someone else that you hope to have yourself. And remember you absolutely have the power to become what you believe. Before you write below, I have to mention that self-like is the vehicle that will drive you to the land of self-love. You can't love yourself and also dislike who you are at the same time. Really do this work, and go beyond the blank spaces below. Consider the following: Would you date you? Would you be your best friend given what you know about who you really are? Ponder those questions until every answer is "yes!"

Write what comes to mind when you ponder the questions below.

Would I date me?

Would I be my best friend?

How?

When?

Why?

What?

Where?

#100WaysToLoveYourself #BelieveBecomeRepeat

ENRICH

1. Know No- Hell yeah! Get to know "no." Say it without guilt or fear, and learn when it's not an option. We can stretch ourselves too thin, trying to please other people, until we have nothing left. I wish that I learned earlier the importance of boundaries— that they are not a bad thing and that the word "NO" is often a necessity. Some people struggle with this particular practice because they are afraid of how it might sound and/or be received; however, there are ways to say it without being rude or polarizing. Just remember to be straightforward because there is no need to beat around the bush. This is your life and sometimes self-love requires this of you. If you are still having an issue with saying "no," please see below.

THEM: I'm working on an album, but we don't have a budget. Can you write a song for my sister's first-cousin's best friend for free?

ME: I won't be able to do it for free, but please ask them to consider me when their budget opens up.

You can apply that scenario to almost any request, and do not be afraid to do it. As an artist, I am OFTEN asked to write or sing for free and the moment I stopped doing it, something interesting happened: they recognized my value and I did too! Try it in your own life, and see what happens!

2. KEEP IT REAL. Authenticity can be challenging. It is far easier to tell someone what they want to hear rather than the hard truth. **Lies are like smoldering embers that can turn into catastrophic wildfires at any given time.** If you find yourself always avoiding conflict with your loved ones, then you may want to rethink their position in your life. When I tell you that I am no expert, I am so serious! Even at this precise moment, as I am writing this book, I grapple with what to even share. I am caught between "keeping it real" and not oversharing. I had to stop a couple times and ponder certain things, and while many revelations will be shared, there are some I'll keep to myself, and that's okay. **Keeping it real doesn't mean that you have to share everything about yourself with the world!** In this sense, it just means being honest in your intentions, as well as being transparent with the ones you love, especially yourself!

3. CHANGE YOUR VIEW. Sometimes you just need to take a step back. It's that simple. You know how a photographer steps back to get the bigger picture? Do that. Take a step back, or a country mile if you need to…whatever it takes to see the bigger picture. Sometimes you can't see clearly when you're too close, or all the way in it, so change the view. Portrait, landscape, traditional, fisheye, or whatever you so desire…it's imperative. Our loved ones can sometimes get nervous when we say that we need space, but **oftentimes clarity comes in isolation,** so don't be afraid to demand your space when you need it. Remember that this is your life and you don't owe anyone an explanation when it comes to getting it together.

4. SLOW YOUR SCROLL. If I wake up and start scrolling through social media before I do anything else, that is my indicator that that something is wrong in real life. Look, I get it! Social media is important. It's the new business card, but do not let it be your god. Sounds ridiculous, I know, but people have actually committed suicide due to the feelings of inadequacy that stemmed from too much engagement in those virtual arenas. **Social media has the power to drastically skew our views and impair our judgment of what is real or not**. More and more, we have grown to accept this expectation of perfection that just isn't possible, and target-marketing will instill insecurities you hadn't even considered before. MY personal remedy for all of that is to monitor myself and limit my time on social media. Engage Rule Number Two and do a massive sweeping. Unfollow and block anyone that does not represent or present peace, love, strength, inspiration, or anything else that brings you joy. I know there are funny memes out there and some are hilarious, but others can be damaging and destructive. If you are on a journey to self-love, then I implore you to really consider this. Some of it seems so trivial and harmless until you reflect on how subconsciously powerful images can be. Think about how destructive and influential propaganda posters have been in the past. This is no different.

So, what I mean by slowing your scroll is to take a step back. Don't let it be the first thing you do, or the highlight of your day. An important take-away from this entire experience is that you may need to take a step back...out of the frame and dissect the picture, but it's nearly impossible to do that while you are in that picture.

5. SET YOUR INTENTIONS, DAILY. It's easier said than done, the action above this one (Slow Your Scroll) will take care of itself if you focus on setting your intentions. In a perfect world, my optimal self would wake up every single morning, and pray and meditate, or as I call it, "medi-pray." After I would medi-pray, I would then connect with the ground in gratitude, open my journal and write my intentions down for the day; however, this is real life and I can't sell perfection if it's not in my stock room. In reality, sometimes I accomplish all of it and sometimes I don't. There are times when I will wake up so upset. The cause of my mood can vary but it sometimes affects my self-image, as well as my progress through the day's activities. Recently, I had one of those mornings. I text my friend, Tiffany, about it and somewhere in the middle of her text she said, "You have to ask yourself, *what is the truth?* The truth is the plans God has for you are good plans of hope to prosper and give you a future...you just have to get in agreement with it." That was it. At that moment, I realized that I wasn't in agreement and, in fact, that will happen sometimes, but we are less likely to fall off of the positivity wagon if we are not steeping in negativity. On normal days, I put my phone down before bed, think about what I want from tomorrow, and before my feet hit the ground, I medi-pray and then on my dry erase board or in my journal, I write down the answers to the same questions.

The repetition of this is where the magic is found. It's the daily practice of stepping inside of ourselves that makes us better people. Not our shoes, hairstyles, or anything else. Life requires that we show up every day with intention and faith that our actions will allow us to experience all of the beauty this life has to offer. But listen, you don't have to do it my way. This is merely guidance and a suggestion, but your way is perfectly fine as long as it stretches and pulls you from the inside until you unearth your soul's deepest beauty. Obviously, every day is not the same and what we do before we close our eyes has everything to do with what happens when we open them. When I woke up in that bad mood, it was because I was having a tough time the night before and I went to sleep that way. I woke up in tears and irritated by everything. It brings a whole new meaning to "I woke up like this." I woke up on the wrong side of the bed as they say because I went to bed consumed by those ill feelings which bled through to the morning. So, now, in concert with setting my intentions daily, one of the most important things that I have found to enrich my life is practicing clearing before I go to bed.

TODAY I AM
GRATEFUL FOR

TODAY I WILL
WALK IN

TODAY I WILL
ATTRACT

TODAY I AM
LETTING GO OF

TODAY I AM
PRAYING FOR

#100WaysToLoveYourself #BelieveBecomeRepeat

Today I am grateful for... Waking up this morning. Thank you for another day.

Today I will walk in.... grace, forgiveness, love, patience and self control

Today I will attract.... mercy, creativity, love, righteousness.

Today I am letting go of – feelings of inadequacy, my past, expectations of others

Today I am praying for – My parents, my siblings, my friends who helped me move, my former property manager's daughter, Olga, for the results of my sister-friends sonogram, better leadership for my country and traveling mercies

6. LET'S BE CLEAR. Rule Number One… do the work. It's simple. No one can do it for you. If the "clean up on aisle one" is in your heart or soul, it will stay a mess until you get the mop and start clearing out the rubbish! **Your spiritual, emotional, and mental house need to be dusted, nurtured, watered, fed, and cleaned, as a daily routine.** Part of that is what I call, clearing. When I lay down at night, to the best of my ability, I visualize myself clearing all of the trash that I have picked up throughout the day. Through this practice, I have learned to:

I am learning to...
CLEAR THE AIR
TO BE CLEAR IN MY INTENTIONS
To be transparent and only accept relationships that are also transparent.
TO BE OPEN AND HONEST WITH MYSELF AND OTHERS.
To clean my spiritual, emotional and mental house daily.

#100WaysToLoveYourself #BelieveBecomeRepeat

The best thing about this is that there is no wrong way to clean, so to speak. I mean, some things are obvious: you don't use the toilet scrubber in the sink, and you only mop after you sweep. Those are basic rules, but when it comes to the end result, the method varies. **Develop your method your way, and then stick to it!** It can be long and drawn out or a simple agreement that you make with yourself in only a few words, thoughts, or actions. Mine is visualization. Like I said, I close my eyes and visualize myself throwing away the things that do not serve me. It prepares me for the day ahead. Yes, "day" ahead because I only take it one day at a time.

As far as relationships go, it is important to be clear about what you want from your romantic partner and what you are willing or unwilling to do in that relationship. Just that little bit of clarity can save both of you so much heartache, time, and resources (and therapy dollars!). Be intentionally clear, not accidentally. One of my visualization exercises includes seeing myself as see-through. I used to think that "clear people" were people who I could see through because they were empty people with no backbone or morals. I wrote about it maybe 15 years ago in a song called "Bullsh*t" (it's funny how we grow), as a sort of a lament of how I felt about the industry and the people at that time: "I can see straight through clear people. Heartless and spineless, trying to fit in. Shielding my joys with pain. Their efforts are all in vain, cause I'm just a gem in this city, trying to maintain."

That was my truth, but over time my view of "clear people" has completely changed. I can still see the heartless coming toward me with fake smiles and promises, but **being clear begets clear** so I see the gold more so now. It was growth that brought me to this point. I was going through hell back then, so maybe all that I could see was the hell in others. What I have learned is that it's our responsibility to be the gold hearts that we want in others. To be the resources that we seek in others. To be the friend; to be the light; to be clear; it will enrich us in a way that money or possessions cannot.

7. CUT TOXIC TIES. Band-aids don't work on infections. I wish that I learned that years ago, but time eventually taught me that lesson. I always put band-aids on friends and relationships, and those band-aids turned into wraps and casts, and those wraps and casts turned into stitches and surgeries, but I never once considered that there was nothing I could do to fix them on the inside. And the truth is that it is all an inside job. If you find yourself constantly trying to fix someone who wants to stay broken, or keeps poisoning you and everyone else, then stop! They are not your responsibility, and if you keep trying to fix them, you will taint yourself in the process. It probably sounds like I am quick to cut someone off, and that's not entirely true. I have been relentlessly loyal to friends and lovers who did not deserve that loyalty or affection, and over time I have developed a mental check-list that protects me from toxic people.... here it is:

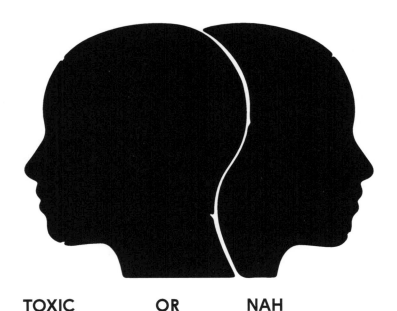

TOXIC   OR   NAH

☐ Judgmental
☐ Self-absorbed
☐ Manipulative
☐ Unreliable yet reliant on you.
☐ Unapologetic
☐ Always says no.
☐ Unsupportive.
☐ Disregards boundaries.
☐ Not responsible for their actions.
☐ Shows up when it benefits them.
☐ Does not listen to you.
☐ Expects you to say yes to all of their requests?
☐ Jealous of you and/or others.
☐ Speaks poorly about others.
☐ Divulges secrets.

☐ Supportive
☐ Loyal
☐ Honest
☐ Apologizes when wrong.
☐ Keeps your secrets.
☐ Uplifts others.
☐ Is reciprocal
☐ Reliable
☐ Make sacrifices
☐ Uplifts you
☐ Listens to you
☐ Respects you
☐ Celebrates you without prompting

#100WaysToLoveYourself #BelieveBecomeRepeat

If you checked off any of the boxes above, then you need to do a friend-check. I call that friendventory.

8. STAND in LOVE. Falling hurts. It implies that you have lost your balance or that you need to be picked up from it. Standing requires strength and fortitude. You have to master standing before you can take steps to walk and move forward towards the life of your dreams. **If you have fallen, pick yourself up and take a stand.** You cannot build or see clearly when you fall; you are flailing about and fighting against the wind. I know we have learned that "falling in love" is one of the ultimate goals in life. You fall in love, get married and have a baby. But standing is also an option. You can do all of those things or none of them...it's your choice. It's your choice to undo broken phrases, words and ideas that no longer serve us. I am standing in love on my own terms, and anything that I do on my own terms that work for me is steeping in fresh warm self-love.

9. **DO THE OPP'!** This has enriched my life so much that I am typing this with the silliest smile on my face. I used to be a person that would sit it out instead of dancing, and the crazy thing is that I always wanted to dance. I was just so broken and couldn't really stand the sight of myself, so I sat down, reaffirming all of the lies that I had been told: *You are not good enough. You are fat. You are disgusting. Nobody likes to see a fat person.* Frankie Beverly would play, and I'd sit there smiling and swaying, all the while picturing myself and how terrible it would be if I got my "fat ass" on the dance floor. Then one day, once I was free... not physically, so to speak, but mentally free, I just got up and danced. And that small act of courage bled light into the endless dark corners of my life. As my friendship grew with my sister-friend Candace, I was faced with the unfathomable challenge of wearing a bathing suit. Not only do I have these scars on my tummy which I hated to explain to people who saw them, but even more than that, I had become this overweight person that I was being conditioned to become (and trust me she tries to make an appearance even now). *Shid*...who am I fooling? She DOES make an appearance every now again, but I fight her like hell and win every time! I also keep her at bay by doing things that she would never do like wearing a bathing suit. I saw Candace and her beautiful family of all shapes and sizes, all happy and enjoying life, and I wanted in!

Then before I knew it, I was "doing the opp" all the time! Doing the opposite will change your pattern, and breathe fresh newness into your entire being. #DOINGTHEOPP

10. **BE YOUR OWN SPECIAL GUEST.** When we are expecting company, we do everything we can to get our dwellings together. We vacuum, mop, dust, put out the good china, cook, and whatever else we can to make our guests feel welcome and comfortable. Well, it is now time for us to show that type of hospitality and attention to ourselves. Although I have begun this next level of practice, this is something that we'll be doing together because it's still a fairly new concept for me as well, and it can be hard to maintain. I had friends over for dinner one Sunday and I went so hard in the paint that I woke up with back pains and muscle engagement, as though I had worked out for hours the day before. What if we went that hard for ourselves? Roll out the red carpet and do everything that you have wanted to do but have been waiting for someone else to do it with or for. Be your own damn knight-in-shining-armor and date yourself! I know you have heard that before, but really consider it. I am currently in a relationship, but I date myself like it's nobody's business. Mask & Mimosas, Movie Night, Self-Appreciation Day…I have done it all. Self-Appreciation Day was born out of a need to make myself feel good about me. I didn't want him to tell me how beautiful and kind I was, or for my parents to shower me in love if I couldn't do the same for myself. I knew that I needed to work on encouraging myself, so I did, and I do, and I always will…even today.

Have you ever cleaned out your car because it was your turn to drive carpool? Or changed your sheets because someone just might spend the night? Or pulled out the good towels and expensive bath soap because your parents are coming to visit? We all have done that or something similar, but right now my challenge to you is to **treat yourself as though you are as important as the most important people in your life** and then act accordingly. You don't have to wait until payday for that either. Here are some ways to treat yourself like a Queen or King on a budget.

TEN WAYS TO TREAT YOURSELF ON A BUDGET

1. Check out an audio book at the library

2 Make your own body scrub

3 Go to a work-shop/event at your place off worship

4 Get a free makeover

5 Make yourself a freezer feast - clean out your freezer by make a meal that's already bought and paid for

6 Save dried flowers and put into a hot bath with essential oils.

7 Go to a local park (alone or with your family).

8 Try a free fitness class

9 Host movie night

10 Eat dessert for dinner

#100WaysToLoveYourself #BelieveBecomeRepeat

EXPLORE

1. JUST DANCE. There is a huge difference between dancing *like* nobody's watching and dancing *WITHOUT* anybody watching. Let me set the mood for you; close your blinds, close your door, turn the music up and go! I split my solo-dance sessions between dancing along to YouTube videos (which sometimes includes instructional line-dancing) and just freestyling to whatever soothes my soul. No slow or nostalgic songs that might evoke the wrong emotion are allowed! This is a different kind of alone time: the kind that can literally free your body and your mind. Exploring yourself is the greatest journey there is, and it doesn't have to always be so serious. Dancing is one of my favorite ways to "go where Taura has never gone." As a bonus, I look up sometimes and a half-hour has passed, but it doesn't feel like I have worked out at all—until the next morning, that is, when I am immediately reminded that going low (*all the way to the flo*) has its consequences. But fear not; with enough of these powerful solo sessions, the soreness will subside, and eventually, you may even develop enough confidence in your own skills to get out there and shake it with a partner, the next time you are at an event or party. Either way, according to a study[10] referenced by Stanford University's Social Dance department, "dancing makes you smarter, longer."[11] So, in addition to potentially increasing confidence and mirroring the benefits of regular exercise, they said that dancing is the only physical activity to offer protection against dementia.

SIDEBAR: You can *#DoTheOpp* with this action as well. I explore different styles of music, line-dances, and all kinds of silly discoveries when I dance by myself. My only partner is usually YouTube, and I, honestly, have the best time. I recommend dancing by yourself because it's so liberating. Sounds silly? Well, try it and then revisit that thought. And don't half-heartedly try it, really commit to it. If the walls of my living room could talk—they wouldn't cause I would have them sign an NDA, but if they could—they would say "Oooh chal', Taura is in here twerking like somebody is paying her to do it!" Yaaas chirred', I twerk, merengue, Zumba, and have also tried Caribbean, African and Latin dances, among others. The cool thing is, I have added a few public moves fresh from my private arsenal. I might learn you something if I ever see you on the dance floor. And speaking of learn ya', I am so intrigued by staying smarter longer, so I am going to commit to dancing at some point in the day, every day. Join me?

2. TOUCH YOURSELF. Self-exploration is the greatest journey of them all, especially when exploring the masterpiece that is the human body. It's miraculous in so many ways! **Our hearts are caged, and our spirits are free!** The tiny joints in our feet carry us, withstanding insurmountable pressure. And our eyes see out into the world and guide us along with our ears and noses to experience what life has to generously offer. When you think of it that way, you have to view it differently. These are not just the hands that need a manicure, they save lives in surgery, paint the atmosphere with music and build the foundations that we stand on. That alone is reason enough to check in with them and make sure all is well. Not just monthly self-breast exams, but in-depth detective work on myself. It usually includes a glass of wine, my phone camera, and various mirrors, but I get the job done, and I want you to do the same! **When we are less of a mystery to ourselves, we are healthier, happier, and fully informed.** And since we're on the subject, touching yourself—as in MASTURBATING—is totally normal for men, women and even my god-dog Huey, is a happy beast and has himself to thank for it. If masturbating makes you a happy beast too, then do it until you are satisfied.

3. INK _____ (your name) INTO YOUR SCHEDULE! Otherwise, you might be tempted to erase it if you only pencil it in. Just before writing this, I was experiencing a roller coaster of emotions; I cried, laughed, and cried again. All of this while my hair was in six braids drenched in deep conditioner, and I had just peeled the last of the black mud mask off of my face (which I am sure is still speckled in some places), but it didn't matter because no one was watching, judging, offended, waiting for me or anything else. In these moments, I medi-pray, contemplate, full-on yell and scream, and whatever else I need to do to get to my breakthrough. The thing about it is that sometimes those breakthroughs happen when I have had a tough day and I am face up on the floor with tears running into my ears, but most times, I set guidelines for my alone time. If not, I will marathon watch anybody from Atlanta with a good wig on TV for hours, and that's okay, sometimes, but **when you want a quality life, you have to do some quality work on yourself.** There are questions that I ask myself that only I can answer, and most times, I need that answer right away. On days like that, I turn off the TV, turn on my meditation music, drink tea, wine, or whatever I want, and I have the deepest conversations with myself. These conversations aren't necessarily intellectually deep, but they are always soul deep! Most times, that quality time coincides with a little of the *Call to Action* above in Number 2 (Touching Yourself), but mostly the quality time that I spend with myself includes guttural cries, grateful reflection, and planning. I do this kind of check-in at least once a month— two- or three-times during months like this, in which I am giving Mercury's retrograde an "F"! The good thing is that I am prepared when I am experiencing a particularly challenging time; I go back to the questions I have already asked myself and I can go over my voice notes or video messages to myself, or even my written plans. To better understand what I mean, see the exercise below.

LEAVE YOURSELF A POSTIVE VOICEMAIL/VOICE NOTE.

LOOK IN THE MIRROR AND SPEAK LIFE INTO AND OVER YOURSELF!

CALL OR VISIT WITH SOMEONE THAT ENCOURAGES YOU!

PRAY AND CONNECT WITH YOUR SOURCE! REMIND YOURSELF THAT YOU ARE...

YOU ARE CAPABLE.

YOU'VE GOT THIS.

YOU ARE BEAUTIFUL INSIDE AND OUT.

YOU ARE NEEDED!

YOU MATTER

YOU ARE LOVED!

#100WaysToLoveYourself #BelieveBecomeRepeat

You can make it as long or short as you need, and on one of those crappy days that we all have, play it back for yourself. You can blast it in your car or play directly into your ears through your headphones. And for the really tough days when you need to sit in front of a friend and see them, you can make a preemptive video. Look into the camera and remind yourself who you are. I can't even type some of the things that I say to myself, because I get all loud and brassy, but guess who sees it? No one. No one sees it but me, and contrary to how silly this exercise may sound, it has helped me climb out of some super dark places and be the light that I was born to be.

4. WAKE A SLEEPING DREAM. I know that we're sometimes told that we were born to do just this one thing, but I don't subscribe to that theory one bit. Just recently I stepped out on the ledge and jumped into unfamiliar waters, and let me tell you, it is warm and beautiful! You are, in fact, holding in your hand the manifestation of a dream that I'd been cultivating since I was 9 years old, writing stories, poetry, and songs in a composition book. I know that doesn't seem too different from writing songs, but trust, it is completely different. I usually write songs alone or with one other person who writes the music. There isn't any input from an editor or artwork to consider. It's also something different about the ability to hold the book in your hand, versus a song, which is held in the heart. Every time someone sends me a DM or tags my first book, I cave because there was a time when I thought that I could never do it, and here I am growing as an author and writer daily. Another dream that I have is to become a content creator and producer and the meetings that I have had to date have blown my mind. I am not better than anyone else in this world, but if you're asking yourself how to wake a sleeping dream, all that I can say is that the more that you weigh the pros and cons, the least likely you will be to manifest one of or all of your sleeping dreams in real life.

I have always been a great cook and my dream is to have my own restaurant. The building blocks to speaking that dream into existence just happened right before your own eyes! The first step is to put it out into the Universe. After that, the next step is to do your research and then get clear on funding and planning. No, it's not easy, and yes there will be obstacles, but like any journey, taking the first step is essential. Don't pigeonhole yourselves into living the dream. **LIVE THE DREAMS.**

SIDEBAR: My beautiful mother is an amazing example of LIVING THE DREAMS. When she lived in Alabama, she did what was expected of a good southern girl back then. She went to school and started working her way toward being a nurse, but she soon realized that dream wasn't hers at all. It was an expectation, and she finally mustered up the courage to tell her family that nursing wasn't an option for her. Soon after, I was hit by a car—more on that later—but she and my dad moved to Oakland, California where she enrolled in cosmetology school and became the talk of the town even before she got her license. She was doing the silk-press decades before it was even a thing. And don't get me started on Jheri-Curls! She was the one that everyone wanted to do theirs, and after years of following one of her dreams, she awoke yet another one, or two. She wanted to be an entrepreneur, to show me and herself that she was, indeed, a boss who could run her own business. That's when Joyful Celebrations was born! That was the name of my Mom's singing telegram and children's party company that not only employed me and my friends but also kept us out of trouble because we were busy being Big Bird or Mickey Mouse on the weekends. She couldn't afford to have all of those costumes made, so she figured out how to make them herself— and they were SPOT ON! In addition to Mickey and Big Bird, she made The Cookie Monster and Minnie Mouse for the kids, and a bouquet of roses, a walking heart, and a birthday cake for her singing telegrams. Let's be honest, I was a teenager back then who didn't know much at all about sacrifice or hard work, but she showed me every single day. She showed me that you can be a good person, love God, live your dreams, live by your talents and still be beautiful and fabulous while doing so. When I was in high school, she performed in San Francisco in an adaptation of Jesus Christ Superstar, and would still wake up first thing in the morning singing praise-music in preparation for her first hair client. She was literally the best example and remains so today. She's constantly reinventing herself, and she still looks beautiful doing it. The big lesson for everyone reading this who has children is to remind you that your kids are watching and soaking up the examples you set like a sponge. And although they may not know it now, when they are ready to squeeze it, everything that you are teaching them will pour out of them.

5. JUMP. It's so much easier said than done, but the truth is, you'll never know until you make a move. Standing still is only helpful to you when you are canvassing the area, but eventually, you just have to jump. By now, most of you have seen the riveting motivational speech that Steve Harvey gave on "Jumping" (and if you haven't, please search for it on YouTube now). He says, "If you are waking up thinking that it's gotta be more to your life than it is… man, believe that it is."[12] I know that's true because I lived that way a great portion of my life. I knew that I wanted more—that I deserved more and that more awaited me, but fear held me captive. It strangled my faith and dared me to hope. I was backed into a corner for many years until I decided that I would jump. I left my four-bedroom house with a pool, recording studio and chef's kitchen to live in someone's extra bedroom. I knew that part would be temporary, but I didn't know what awaited me after that. I just knew that I had to go. So, my co-worker's husband drove out to help me on a rainy day. We loaded his pickup truck with all that could fit, and that wasn't much. Other than my guitar, some pots and pans, clothes, and a few other things, I didn't have anything left. I had a great job as Paris Hilton's personal assistant, and what a soft landing from one of many jumps that I had to take during that time period. I was still picking up the pieces that were shattered inside of me, for years. I told this story in more detail in the first book, so please refer to it because I don't want to unearth something that I have happily buried, again and again. I will admit, however, that I didn't seek appropriate counseling at the time, so I ended up having the same sort of relationship all over again, with an even bigger monster. But then I geared up and prepared for my next jump. I was going to take a job for an executive who worked mostly in Florida. I would have spent most of my time there and would have made three times the money that I was making with Sean Combs, who I worked for briefly following my job with Paris Hilton. It felt wrong because I knew that I would be abandoning my purpose, but the money was so right. I have since learned to never let money be a motivation for choices that could change the landscape of my life. It had to be rooted in something deeper. My co-writer Raphael saw my struggle and made me an offer that I couldn't refuse. He told me to bet on myself and work for him in the studio during the day and we would write together at night. When he said that he could only pay me $12 per hour, I almost jumped in the other direction, but I was committed to moving forward, closer to my dream of becoming a well-respected songwriter. So, although I was scared, I jumped anyway. I wondered how I would take care of myself, pay rent or even have money for gas in Los Angeles on $12 per hour. However, I honestly believe that when you jump and meet God halfway, He will meet you there and make it all make sense. The first meeting with God happened when one of Raphael's producers had to move out of the building next door to the studio. He asked if I wanted to move out of my apartment—which was cute enough but had questionable plumbing, paper-thin walls and was in a seedy part of town—to the apartment that he was going to still be responsible for the duration of the year lease that had about ten months left on it. Of course, I said yes, and moved into the building directly adjacent to his studio. I no longer had to worry about gas because I walked to work, or rent because he allowed me to pay what I was paying at the other apartment, which was about 75% of the rent. Although it was still tough making only $12 per hour, God met me again: I was called by two people for the same job. Nia Hill called to say that she was partnering with a notable person to release music for her TV show, Sunday Best, and she thought I'd be an excellent A&R rep. Days later, Matthew Knowles called to offer me the A&R job for Music World in connection to Sunday Best. Those two calls helped take care of me financially and also gave Raphael and me the space that we needed to step away and come back fresh and ready to write. None of that would have happened if I would have stayed on the ledge.

If you are on the ledge now, I implore you to jump. You will never know how it feels to be whole if you stay in a place that leaves you feeling empty. If you are scared, you are on the right track, because the act of jumping without knowing where you will land can be incredibly unnerving. Every single time that I jump, I am terrified. I mean absolutely terrified, but I just do it, anyway. A few years ago, I had the opportunity to write a song about it that won Best Song in a Documentary at the Critics' Choice Awards, and the HMMAs as well. It was featured in the film *Step* that was scored by the incredible Laura Karpman and Raphael Saadiq. They asked me to write for this emotional moment when against all odds, the girls from the Baltimore Leadership School for Young Women's step team were graduating from high school. I usually write down a collection of thoughts before writing a song, but these thoughts poured out in full sentences. Likely because it was instructional and just a retelling of what I had been through time and time again. I poured my heart into every word alongside Raphael and Laura, who beautifully wrote the music and, together, we created a song that I hope can be the theme song for jumping. If you are considering taking a leap, then I hope that one listen will propel you into your greatest self.

JUMP

Don't look down
Feel the sound
of your heartbeat daring loud
It's not brave, if you're not afraid…
to set darkness ablaze and light up blind faith
You've gotta jump..
Go jump

Jump
Cause the whole worlds waiting
Jump
No more hesitating
Jump – Jump
Oh Jump
Who you wanna be is born in the leap …
Jump –Jump
Jump
When your knees are shaking
Jump
When your heart is racing
Jump-Jump
Oh Jump
There's no guarantees that
That you'll land on your feet but
Jump
Go Jump

You must fight
Just like her
The one that knows your worth
At your best and your worse..
She's there.
Show here you care.
The mirror is your oldest friend
She won't let you pretend..
She'll push you to no end..
Right then is when you jump.

To get to the other side
Jump
To know how it feels to fly
Jump
Together we can go higher
Stronger, deeper like wild fire
Even though the world is colder
Jump
You can stand on my shoulder
You can't keep sitting down
Get up, spread your magic all around
It's not brave if you're not afraid.
Trust the light that leads the way.
You've gotta fight if you wanna win.
If you fall, get up and jump again.

Written by Raphael Saadiq, Taura
Stinson and Laura Karpman

6. **DIG.** I read a quote by an unknown author that said: "Keep digging, you may only be three feet away from gold." The truth is that **if you are digging for gold, you need look no further than inside yourself.** True story. We all have actual gold inside of us. According to *TheBlackDoctor.com*, we each contain about 0.2 milligrams of gold, mostly in our blood. It has also been widely reported that the gold found in our blood is concentrated around our hearts.[13] And if that doesn't wow you, consider this: we are also "remnants of stars,"[14] according to National Geographic, and yet most of us don't even know that. It's fascinating to learn that we carry precious metals and minerals inside of us, yet we look to outside sources to find our shine. It is inside of you. In *I Know Why the Caged Bird Sings*, Maya Angelou writes, **"There is no greater agony than bearing an untold story inside of you."**[15] Some of you don't think you have a story. On many occasions, an old friend had said to me, "I feel like I don't have a story because nothing bad has happened to me." I implored her to dig deeper until she hit the nerve connected to that limiting thought, and I'm sure she'd find her story, and that the story wouldn't necessarily be a bad one. So many people think, that our stories are filled with trials and tribulations, without realizing that we build many of them on solid ground, and those stories need to be heard, too.

If we live on the surface, all we get are sediments and diluted versions of the richness found when we dig down into the core of who we truly are. The deeper you go, the dirtier you may get, but the dirt is proof that you have been in the trenches, and it takes having been in the trenches to know what it's like to have come out of them.

7. **INTERVIEW YOUR ELDERS.** My Grandma Mittie Morton passed when I was around five or six years old, but I still remember the advice that she left behind. She said, "God gave us two ears and one mouth for a reason." I later learned that the logic behind that is that we should listen twice as much as we speak. I come from a family that has evolved since I was a kid. There were no children's rights or anything progressive like that. The rules were pretty much

like this: **Stay out of grown folks' business. The end.** So, when I visited Alabama and my mom and her sisters sat around the table playing cards and talking, I was expected to at least pretend that I didn't know what was going on. Things have changed now. Nobody is getting whoopin's anymore, and kids talk back with curse words. If I even thought about cursing to either of my parents, I would be writing this book from heaven right now. I don't resent them one bit for it, because my cousins and I developed world-class ear hustlin' abilities by listening through concrete walls, 80s R&B bass, and bones (dominoes) being slammed on the table. We learned how to navigate so much by listening and not saying a word, but now I am an adult who is blessed to have both of my parents and Grandma Grace, my 90-year-old grandmother, and more than a dozen aunts and uncles (combined) to draw from. In those moments when I am visiting Alabama, or even just on one of my long phone conversations with my grandma, I still mostly just listen. I ask a question or two about her upbringing and different stages of her life and she "spills the beans," as she calls it. She lost one of her ten children to gun violence over fifty years ago. My father was standing right next to him when it happened. It was important for me to listen to how he was affected by that experience because although I struggled with his absence for most of my childhood, I was able to better understand him as a person and more clearly see how his brother's death impacted him and his actions thereafter.

There are so many ways to guide the conversations with our elders and starting with basic information is always a good start. I called my grandma recently and asked several questions about herself (see questions below). Her responses led to a two-hour conversation that went far beyond the confines of the questions asked. Some of them weren't even answered, and that's okay because it started a dialogue that I can springboard from every time that we talk. If you don't have loving parents or grandparents, that's okay—knowledge and wisdom aren't limited exclusively to bloodlines.

ELDER CONVERSATION STARTER

How was life for you when you were my age?

_____

_____

What about younger?

_____

_____

What's the biggest lesson that life has taught you?

_____

_____

Any regrets?

_____

_____

#100WaysToLoveYourself #BelieveBecomeRepeat

8. REEVALUATE YOUR RELATIONSHIPS. This is a necessary pain, because all of your ships may not stay afloat. Some of your friendships will sink to the bottom, even some of the ones you thought would ride into the sunset with you. This past year was super tough for me with friendships. I had to let one go because it was one-sided. Period. That was the reason. Any ship that carries all of the weight on one side will eventually capsize. I admit that, like every one of you reading this, I am not perfect, but I pride myself on being a stellar friend. Given that I don't have children or any nearby family here in LA, my friends are a huge part of my life. I usually say yes to what is asked of me and I go above and beyond to make sure my friends are good, but after years of non-reciprocal interactions, I finally had to walk away. It hurts to this day, but it's something that I had to do for myself because it started to show up in other areas of my life. The old adage, "what you allow will continue," is a truth that I have had to remind myself of often. While we journey toward the goal of loving ourselves, we have to clear away some debris out of the water, otherwise, it will undoubtedly resurface somewhere down the line. That doesn't mean that I don't love this person or even that we can't possibly be friends again in the future, but like Lauryn Hill's lyrics: "Tell me, who do I have to be to get some reciprocity?"[16] I have to laugh about it sometimes to keep from crying, but I am proud of myself for taking a stance. We can paint a picture of this amazing human being that looks good on paper, but in reality, is where it counts and my quest for self-love requires me to call everyone to the carpet, including myself. I recently experienced another loss of friendship. Someone else who I love deeply, disconnected from me for sharing what I thought was a trivial detail with a dear mutual friend. Although I apologized profusely, I soon realized that they didn't care to hear from me. This made me angry, and although it may not have necessarily been the right reaction, it felt warranted. We never had any major disagreements, and we were in a reciprocal, supportive friendship for over twenty years. So, my thought was that maybe they were harboring ill feelings towards me all along. That's the only thing that made sense to me, but the crux of this is that I should never have, no matter how trivial it seemed to me, shared anything with anyone about that friend's situation. So, I had to give this friend what they wanted, and that was not to talk to me. I am being transparent because with love, it's the only way. The friend in the first scenario offended me, and I offended the friend in the second scenario. I love them both, but the vessels need to be fixed before they can sail again. The gem in the ocean of sinking friendships, however, is that I still have lasting friendships that date back to the fifth grade, as well as a few newer ships that I am sure will stand the test of time. Obviously, those are not the only ships in the sea. We have non-platonic relationships to consider too, and I can honestly write an entire book on that. I spent many years in non-reciprocal relationships and was made to feel like I didn't deserve love; and I believed that whole-heartedly, thus I accepted what was given to me. Nowadays, I know my worth and won't accept anything less. I reevaluate my romantic relationship with more scrutiny than most because I refuse to go back to the mind-state that I was previously stuck in.

Lastly, while you are at it, be sure to include your family in your reevaluation process. Blood does not guarantee reciprocity, and that, my friends, is non-negotiable when it comes to a healthy relationship of any kind. When you learn or are learning to love yourself, you will require more from those that say that they love you.

9. Be Still. Some of the biggest revelations in my life have come in those moments when I am still. In those moments I am usually depleted and in desperate need of answers, and God never fails to deliver on His promises. I pepper those promises all throughout this text, but this one is fresh, as it just happened in me. I say "happened in me" because it was spirit to spirit. Mine and the divine's, to which I am miraculously connected. I was flipping through a journal that reads "But First Pray" on the front. I opened it, with my pen in hand, ready to write the next prayer, but instead decided to read the first one that I had written about a year earlier. In it, I thanked God for my former landlord, Ms. Olga who charged me far less than I should have paid for rent. I got the sense that she believed in me and wanted to see me do well. In my last apartment, I had sticky notes all over the place, but in the living room where I worked mostly, there was one that said: "This place is temporary, you will have another one soon." Well, in that book, I was about to write a 'woe-is-me' prayer like, "Do you hear me, God? Where are you?" But then after seeing the prayer that I had written about my landlord, coupled with the sticky note about my place being temporary, I realized then that I was actually comfortably sitting in a prayer answered. Reading a prayer from the other side of the answer is something that I rejoice in, even when I just think of it, it brings me joy. I was in a place with everything that I asked for in that prayer, and the stillness led me to that finding.

For me, I find stillness in writing. It's second nature and gives me the peace I so desperately need sometimes. Being still does not actually mean sitting there without movement, at least not to me, anyway. It means to move naturally in your own language where you and your source connect. My mind is open to receive all messages from love when I am in a state of prayer or gratitude. And just in case the stillness falls into chaos and disorder, I look down to find another answered prayer. **Find your stillness and meet God there. I guarantee you that He will not be a no-show.**

10. FIND YOUR TELLURIDE! The concept of travel for some is nearly impossible, and I have totally been there, but if you can think of ways to trim your budget to make room even for a quick getaway, DO IT! I am very blessed to live in California where majestic beauty surrounds us; you can literally go from the beach straight to a ski lodge in the same day! Although you may not have the beach, I am willing to bet that there are adventures, beautiful landscapes, and historical treasures right at your backdoor. I have seen this firsthand while touring with Ryan Bingham. This will sound silly, but I really had no idea how beautiful this country is! We recently visited Telluride, Colorado and fell in love. I wondered if everyone living in Denver who wants a beautiful vacation has been there? If not, no matter where you are, put it on your list of places to go. There are gondolas that take you over a beautiful enchanted forest and then you land on a mountaintop town with beautiful restaurants, crisp air, and views that you wouldn't believe. Candace and I walked on the cobblestone streets through the farmers market to the best tacos at night and breakfast in the morning. Thankfully, the tour helped me to discover this foreign native land because it encouraged me to find the gems in my own backyard. I'm always saving for that big trip to Italy or some exotic island, and although I have been to both and highly recommend traveling abroad, I also think it's equally important to get to know what's in your own backyard. The idea is to explore the parts of you that respond to your environment.

In Telluride, I discovered that elevation sickness is manageable if you prepare for it. A month earlier, I had extreme elevation sickness after visiting the Red Rocks in Colorado because I just wasn't prepared for the altitude. But after a few Google searches for tips to avoid elevation sickness before our next trip, I was able to take full advantage of my Telluride experience. If you're curious about what I did to prepare, I pretty much didn't drink wine, as I had previously, and for the first time ever, I purchased a huge can of oxygen! We were only there a couple of days, but everything about it felt bigger, wider, and deeper. Even our hotel (Camel's Garden) was the perfect getaway with The Aveda Spa and the huge tubs where I soaked away my aches and troubles every morning and night. One of the more practical take-aways from the beautiful hotel were the humidifiers. Every room had one, and since it was there, I filled it with water and, voilà, no more dryness. I have since implemented this practice into my daily life. That one exploration and adventure added something that has become priceless for me. Getting to Telluride for the weekend isn't the easiest trek from LA, but we do have Big Bear: a place where I'll see if I can grab a star and put it in my pocket like I did in Telluride. Sorry for the rant, but this place had a huge impact on me, and I can only hope that you all find that feeling in a place near you.

According to the Global Coalition on Aging, studies showed that men and women who did not vacation regularly had a "significantly higher risk of developing a heart attack or coronary death" or "risk of death from heart disease."[17] It doesn't have to be an extravagant vacation, just go somewhere for a day! My go-to for many years is Palm Springs. It's only a two-hour drive from LA, but it feels otherworldly and satisfies my need to break the monotony. Sometimes I even break free by staying within county lines, and just packing up a bag and going to the beach or for a hike in our beautiful mountains. I hope you will go out and find your getaway now too. It's good for your health!

SIDEBAR: I was sitting outside taking in the view when I saw Gary Shapiro. He and I are both members of the Academy of Motion Pictures Arts and Sciences, and we usually only see one another at screenings during Oscar season. He and his wife Jane are always so amazing, and we usually end up chatting and planning to catch up. They are such a joy! LA tends to be the kind of place where people welcome you with open arms at one event and pretend not to see you the next— but they are always the same, warm, funny and #goals! Gary told me that Jane was inside and as I ran in to greet her, it hit me that her artwork was all over the hotel. I marveled at it but didn't put the two together until that moment. They ended up coming to The Blues Festival that we performed at and we all had a beautiful breakfast the next morning with Gary & Jane at the helm of stories that felt made us feel like we were thrust into an 80s film with Warhol and Basquiat, Jane, Gary and all of the super-cool artistic people of that time. They were in Telluride because they purchased a home there many years ago before they even purchased their home in LA. Gary credits Jane for that wise decision, and even now she is seemingly city-miles ahead of us all! They are both a sheer joy, and as a gift to you, I asked Jane if she could share one of her pieces with you, and she said yes! Below is a black and white version of one of her window pieces at the hotel in Telluride. If you want to see it in color, you must go to the mountain ☺ Add your own vibrant colors to it and be sure to tag Jane on Instagram. @JaneGoren

Here's that mirror again... Before we start the next chapter, please draw another self-portrait.

#BELIEVEBECOMEREPEAT #100WAYSTOLOVEYOURSELF

MANIFEST

1. Start With A Grateful, Connected Heart. I strongly encourage you to get a gratitude/prayer journal. It puts things into perspective and quite frankly monitors some of our desires. It's hard to write down, "God, can you just please give me a Benz." I think of that every time I drive by someone who is struggling to make it up the street with bags in one hand and hopelessness in the other. When I was a little girl, my mom would routinely give women rides that were at the bus stop. Her heart was and continues to be wide open to help without any expectation in return. Sometimes I let my fear speak for me and say, "Really, Mom? What if she has a gun or a knife?" In response, she would pray for a hedge of protection around us, and keep walking or driving in her purpose. I am thankful for those moments when those seeds were being planted into my being; I now have a heart of service because I was raised by a woman with one. That does not mean that you can't have one as well, even if your circumstances were different. You just have to get in the practice of connecting to your source and shining the light inside you, out into the hearts of those who need it most.

I don't have a set time when I write in my journal, but once you're in the practice of giving thanks, your heart will nudge you to submit that beautiful memory, person, or outcome to your written recollection of gratitude. I have carved out a few pages to get you started for a few days. Keep in mind that it can either be a sentence or enough to fill the four pages that follow. Just stay connected and pour your heart out with thanks and prayer/meditation.

#100WaysToLoveYourself #BelieveBecomeRepeat

2. Believe. It's a process that no one can do for you. As much as your parents, significant other or dog loves you, they cannot *believe* for you. I know it's hard sometimes, but you have two choices: You can either be a believer or an unbeliever in yourself. I used to talk myself out of the best opportunities simply by not believing that I had a right to be there. Now when I walk into the room where Oprah's to my left and Quincy Jones is to my right (literally), I center my thoughts and close the door on any negative thoughts. I engage Rule Number 5 (Speak Life) and stand in my own greatness. If there are non-believers in your midst, they have gots to go! I mean seriously. The truth is that you can do all of this work, but if you have someone constantly telling you that you are in the wrong room or that you should try it their way, or that you have not even a clue, you are going to have to schedule their season finale (and possibly cancel that series altogether). **You cannot afford to be tainted by a "can't."** That word and other negative words will creep up on you every now and again, but you have to stop them before they take up residence in your heart and mind. I am still learning not to self-deprecate. Saying things like "this is too hard," "they will never-," "I will never-," or "I want to give up," are all blasphemous to the God in you. You are capable and here for the reasons that no one can own but you. What you believe, you will receive. I stand on that theory every day, but an important component of that lifestyle is to come from an honest place. **You can't be diligent in the 'believe-become-repeat' lifestyle while speaking ill of (or not wishing the best for) your brother or sister.** You can't have a whole mess of trash lying on your bedroom floor, saying "look at this spotless living room." Clean it all up and come from a whole place and your manifestations will mirror that. It takes hard work, but so does anything that's worth having. You will get there, to a place where you really 'believe' and when you do, continue, because the process repeats itself in cycles unknown.

3. Have What You Think. I have touched on this briefly already, but I wanted to dedicate a *Call to Action* to changing the ways that you think. I am in constant conversation with myself, correcting thoughts before they even make it out of my mouth, and I highly recommend it. The cycle is simple: **thoughts become words, words become declarations and declarations become reality.** Therefore, it is important that you guard your thoughts with all that you have. Another important lesson I learned is 'reframing'. We are in the picture, and that does not change, but sometimes reframing that picture can change the way that you see it. Pulling the positives out of negative situations has was the most challenging part of my continued growth process, but I always work towards it because changing perspectives often makes all the difference. I read an article on the Johns Hopkins Medicine website in which they perfectly described the best way to practice reframing: "Instead of stressing about the traffic jam, for instance, appreciate the fact that you can afford a car and get to spend a few extra minutes listening to music or the news, accepting that there is absolutely nothing that you can do about the traffic."[18] I love how they turned what some view as a negative into a positive. If you need help with this, I offer this: instead of stressing about your relationship and wondering if your partner is being faithful to you, take a moment to consider how amazing you are and accept the fact that you cannot change anyone but yourself. Instead of beating yourself up because you gained a couple of pounds, be thankful that you have faith in yourself and know that you are fully capable of doing whatever you put your mind to. Reframing is necessary, and so is thinking positively. I am often wrestling negative thoughts to the floor of my brain, and sometimes they come back, but believe me they are less powerful with every visit, and before I know it, they are gone. However, you have to be careful because they can show up as small thoughts and before you know they are blaring loud and drowning out every ounce of goodness inside of you. That is why it's necessary to feed your mind good food in the form of good podcasts and/or books that speak to you. Not every author is for every reader. I have a friend who wasn't a big reader until she found *You are a Badass* by Jen Sincero. She blew through it in two days and then read it again (something that she hadn't done before) because it spoke to her. Find a voice that breaks through all of the stuff going on inside of your mind and gives you the feeling that you matter.

4. Hold It. By "it" I mean, your belief. Hold it in prayer or meditation. Affirm it by setting your intention straight up to face the light that is coming for it. If this is a foreign concept, it's okay. You'll get the hang of it because it's so much easier than it sounds. If you're old school, then refer to the days when they would say "Name it, claim it! It's Yours!" Because **if it is yours, and you see it first in your mind, then the Universe and the God of the Universe will open doors for you that no man can shut but you!** Doubt is our own worst enemy and it can poison every clear intention that we set in stone and make it crumble to the ground.

5. Write It Down. This is an extension of Numbers 3 and 4 of this section and for me, it's a fundamental part of the process. Once you condition your mind to not let doubt or pessimism take up residence there, you have to write down the basis of what you are going to manifest, and really consider what it will require of you. Everything in life has a cause and effect. So, if your future manifestation is going to cause someone else harm, or is at all done with malicious intent, just know that you are actually manifesting that for yourself. Check your intentions and clear your energy and your soul of negativity, ill will, or anything that does not represent this beautiful, empowered, and empowering person you are on your way to being.

Start small. Write down something that you will be doing six months from now and sign your name to signify that you are in agreement with it and then watch what happens. If it's good and pure, it will not return to you void. So, here you go… Feel free to write it down in the space below and come back to report your progress.

_____
_____
_____
_____
_____
_____
_____
_____
_____
_____
_____
_____
_____
_____
_____
_____
_____
_____
_____
_____
_____
_____
_____

#100WaysToLoveYourself #BelieveBecomeRepeat

6. Give Not to Receive. Giving and receiving are both rooted in the same soil. This comes from the same place as making sure your intentions are pure. A perfect example of this is that I recently organized my bathroom and cleaned out my closet. As a result, I purged some of my masks, scrubs, and facial products. Anyone who knows me knows how important skincare is to me, so at first, it was not easy, and they just stayed right in the bag until I got myself together. The goal was to walk by the bag and not want to rummage through it one more time. It took a few days, but finally, I was clear and in the space that I wanted to be in while giving those things away. I also got rid of clothing and tons of shoes. Shoes that I swear that I loved, but I would never take out on the town. When my friend came over to get the bag of facial products, she was stunned. She said that "some really, really good things were in that bag," and then joked about me making space for awesome things to come. Literally days later, a friend called me. She works with a certain superstar who was on tour and said she had shoes for me (and when she has shoes for me, they are SHOES-SHOES!). It was so timely because after that another friend called to invite me to BeautyCon. I had never been, so I thought, Cool, this will be nice—but I kid you not, we left there with so many bags that it rivaled the Oscar Awards-gifting. I was able to disperse beauty products to all, like "you get a palette, and you get a palette!" The real gold in this story is that I was given what I gave away, plus more. But first I had to correct the intention with which I was giving.

One day, I saw a woman as I was leaving a busy restaurant. She was sitting on a walker, with a Veterans sign. The traffic was horrendous, and I was forced to turn, but I drove around several city blocks just to give her the twelve dollars that I had in my purse. In return, she told me that she loved me, and I believed her. I had no intention of receiving change or glory from her or anything else. It was pure and completely love-filled. I walked away thinking that I want all of my giving to feel exactly like that.

7. See Yourself Whole. This is a biggie for me because there was a time when I could not picture myself. I would go and look in the mirror and sort of see myself reflected, but not really, so without a mirror, I could only envision a terrible version of myself. Each time I pictured myself, I would see someone twice as heavy, with her head down and looking as though the slightest sound would shatter me to my core. This went on for years. I saw the person that I was told I was every day until I started to push her out. It happened when I found a picture of me. The person I was before him; I looked great, and although that was nice, what I remembered the most was how happy I was and how much I used to laugh. This was a stark contrast from the person I had become—sad and crying, sometimes four times a day. To keep from really doing something terrible to myself, I would close my eyes and visit the old me. Before I knew it, I was returning to that happy version of myself and there was no longer any room for that smaller person I was never meant to be in the first place. If you want not to be sick, you have to see yourself as healthy. If it's a relationship, you have to see yourself as whole and then connecting with another whole person. **There is no such thing as a better half. Align with your better whole.**

8. Vision Board *(Grinding on that 'Would')*. Speaking of a "Better Whole," where will you live? What will you do for a living? How will you help to change the world? Will you have children? The great thing about vision boards is that you can put whatever you want on them as long as it is an accurate depiction of your future. A misconception is that we all have the same vision. Your vision may be stimulated by magazine cut-outs, while mine may be sentences on a dry-erase board. Either way, they are both boards, holding our respective visions. I highly recommend creating one in a way that isn't influenced by anyone else and then go to bed and wake up to it every night and day. Over time, it becomes embedded in your psyche, and that's when the pieces of that vision will start to manifest!

9. Dream Big. One of my favorite quotes from Oprah is, "Create the highest, grandest vision of your life, because you become what you believe."[19] That hits differently coming from a black billionaire, media and wellness mogul who is also a WOMAN. And like many women from that era, Oprah had to kick down doors and swim through a sea of "no's" just to get her hand on the one "yes" that all kinds of black girls like her were reaching for. We have made tremendous progress since then, especially in the last five years. Inclusion and diversity are two words that are being forced down the throats of chauvinists, racists, and classists. As a result, women of color are taking their seats at the table! We have a long way to go, but we are going, and it shows in the children. Little girls now say they want to write like Lena Waithe, be a lawyer and writer like Michelle Obama, a powerful CEO like Indra Nooyi, or an Academy Award-nominated songwriter like Taura Stinson. The title doesn't define me by any means, but it does put a huge gold star on the years of sacrifice and hardships I have faced in this industry. I frequently saw people give up, but I didn't speak that language. I dreamt my way from one phase to the next, and when I saw Halle Berry win an Oscar, I was so proud, but it did something to me to learn that she was the first black woman to win for Best Actress. I thought it was a typo. I then started to prepare my mind for a shift in thinking and being. I started early in film, having written the first released song ever for Destiny's Child on the *Men in Black* soundtrack, so I shifted my focus back to films on a new quest to become an Oscar-winning songwriter. Then somewhere along that journey, I allowed a limiting thought to take residence, and I put my dream on hold. By the time I picked it up again, I had minimized my dream to more simply becoming an Oscar-nominated songwriter. And because we become what we believe, I am now an Oscar-nominated songwriter—but the next time you see me there, know that I have held the grandest vision for my life and I KNOW that I will become an Oscar & Golden-Globe Award-winning songwriter. My dream was too small, but life has taught me over and over to dream big, and I am listening!

10. SURRENDER. It's easier to say than it is to do, and oftentimes we undo so much good, necessary work by rushing the process. **If you fan a photo while it's developing, the quality is compromised.**

The same thing happens when you try to rush your own process. Steep in it. Sit in the dark and hold your negatives up to the light. Learn from it and rest in it. Surrender to the process. When I was a kid they would sing, "I Surrender All" as the altar-call song. It went on for ages while the pastor waited for everyone to make their way to the pulpit to simply lay their burdens on the cross and, as they would say, surrendering to Christ. The lyrics are simple: "I surrender all. I surrender all. / All to thee my blessed savior. I surrender all."[20] It's vulnerable, sacred, and paints this picture of surrendering being a necessary passage to your higher self. The lyrics to our Oscar-nominated song, "Mighty River" starts with "Life is a Teacher. Time is a healer." I could write those words only because I was broken wide open and healing was the only way, or else I would not be on this earth. This is the same for Mary J. Blige, who was nominated alongside me and became the first person ever to be nominated for Best Original Song and Best Actress. Now, that's a warranted and notable first. She recorded vocals the night before her first divorce proceeding. The pain was so thick that you could scoop it. But the process rendered both of us whole. We had to go through very similar experiences, and it was no mistake that our worlds would collide at the edge of our surrender.

MIGHTY RIVER

Life is a teacher
Time is a healer
And I'm a believer
Like a river wild

Ego's a killer
Greed is a monster
But love is stronger...
Stronger than them all

White flag in hand
I don't wanna fight
No lines in the sand
I'm on your side
Invisible
No color lines
It's time we put our (put our, put our)
Differences aside.

Time tells no lies
It keeps changing and ticking and moving then passes by.
But if you're lucky
It will be kind
Like a river
Flowing through time

Like a river
Let it wash u clean
Mighty river
Going up stream
Like a river
Cutting through rock
Mighty river
Cause it never gives up
Like a river

So full of life
Mighty river
Liquid like time
Like a river
Let it wash away
Mighty river
The pain from yesterday

Love is the answer
Hate is a cancer
Oh, but forgiveness.
It waters the soul.
Our blood is red, we're not so different…
Cause underneath our skin, we're identical.
White flag in hand
I don't wanna fight
No lines in the sand
I'm on your side
Invisible
No color lines
It's time we put our (put our, put our)
Differences aside.
We know wrong from right

LIKE A RIVER
Let it wash you clean
MIGHTY RIVER
Going up stream
LIKE A RIVER
Cutting through rock
MIGHTY RIVER
Cause it never gives up
Like a river
So full of life
Mighty river
Liquid like time
LIKE A RIVER
Let it wash away
The pain from yesterday

AFFIRM

Affirmations are served best in the way that resonates with you. For me, repetition and frequency are everything. So, in a meditative style, I affirm, and reaffirm extraordinary possibilities and future realities to my subconscious mind. Sometimes I recite my affirmations in the mirror while doing my makeup, but more often than not, my affirmations are spoken following moments of gratitude, before my feet even touch the ground. Frankly, it keeps me sane. Years ago, I had "Believe-Become" tattooed on my forearm so that I would constantly be reminded that my thoughts are fully capable of becoming my future. That remains helpful to me when I am faced with an invasive thought that doesn't serve my growth. Sometimes they stick around a few hours, and then I'll catch a glimpse of my tattoo and remember that the power to change the trajectory of the next second, minute, day, week, month, year, and future is within me.

The Merriam-Webster Dictionary defines self-affirmations as "the act of <u>affirming one's</u> own worthiness and value as an individual for beneficial effect (such as increasing one's confidence or raising self-esteem)."[21] I couldn't have said it better. In short, I firmly believe that self-affirmations have made all of the difference in my life. There were times that I didn't know my worth at all. I mean, AT ALL. Putting the responsibility in someone else's hands is so dangerous, and that's exactly what I did. As a result, I found myself staring down the barrel of a gun once, and another time being within seconds of losing my breath—I felt it slipping away and saw bits of black speckles peppering my view. Never had I seen that before, and I knew in that moment that I had to decide between giving in to the darkness or using the little strength I had left to fight. I chose to fight, and ever since that day, I slowly but surely learned that saying is believing. I spoke myself free; literally standing in the mirror every morning and saying, "You deserve the best." That was the first self-affirming thought I remember saying to myself, over and over again, until I actually believed it. I was my own experiment, and it worked! I know there are skeptics out there, but if you made it this far into this book, then I hope that you are open to the idea that your mind can heal your body, change your view of yourself, change your reality and free you from bondage.

The next ten affirmations are made to be cut out of this book. Cut along the perforated lines and tape them to your mirror, or the first place you look when you wake up in the morning, or on the dash of your car (but don't read while driving). Preceding each affirmation is a centering thought by some of the world's greatest teachers. On the blank pages on the backside of each affirmation is space for you to write your own affirmation. Please share them with me when you do.

"We are stars trapped in skin-the light
you are seeking has always been within"
- Rumi

I am a light source that
shines from the inside out. All
of the power that I need to
create a life immersed in reciprocal love is inside of me.

I believe it, and it is so!

#100WaysToLoveYourself   #BelieveBecomeRepeat

"So I say to you: Ask and it will be given to you; seek and you will find; knock and the door will be opened to you."
-Matthew 7:7

No one can close the doors that are opening for me. I am divinely guided and spiritually connected to the source of all beings. *I believe it, and it is so!*

#100WaysToLoveYourself #BelieveBecomeRepeat

"Nothing will work unless you do."
Maya Angelou

I am strong, capable and committed to doing the work required to manifest abundance.

I will continue to plant seeds in preparation for a bountiful harvest in ALL areas of my life!

I am committed to the growth process and I am becoming the person that I always believed I would be.

I believe it, and it is so!

#100WaysToLoveYourself #BelieveBecomeRepeat

"I found God in myself and I love her".

- Ntozake Shange

I am a sacred place.

I AM SACRED.

I am a source of healing.

I AM HEALED.

Love pours into and out of me.

I AM LOVE.

I believe it, and it is so!

#100WaysToLoveYourself #BelieveBecomeRepeat

"The primary cause of unhappiness is never the situation but thought about it. Be aware of the thoughts you are thinking. Separate them from the situation, which is always neutral.

— Eckhart Tolle

I am in complete control of my mind and aware that happiness, and peace starts there.

I choose to be happy regardless of my circumstances, rejoicing in the fact that I woke up this morning. That is a privilege not reserved for all.

I am grateful for another day to become my absolute best self.

I will nurture my mind and spirit with seeds of peace, knowledge, happiness and wisdom…all rooted in love.

I believe it, and it is so!

#100WaysToLoveYourself #BelieveBecomeRepeat

Darkness cannot drive out darkness: only light can do that. Hate cannot drive out hate: only love can do that."
– Dr. Martin Luther King Jr.

I am a light source that shines from the inside out. All of the power that I need to create a life immersed in reciprocal love is inside of me.

I believe it, and it is so!

#100WaysToLoveYourself #BelieveBecomeRepeat

We are shaped by our thoughts; we become what we think. When the mind is pure, joy follows like a shadow that never leaves.
— Buddha

Today I acknowledge my limitless self-worth I am worthy.
Today I acknowledge my strength and resilience. I am strong and resilient.
Today I am grateful to be here on earth. I am present.
Today I honored to share this human experience with likeminded people on the on a similar path to enlightenment and I reject anything or anyone not rooted in love, peace, positivity and growth.

I believe it, and it is so!

#100WaysToLoveYourself #BelieveBecomeRepeat

"When you attempt something new, there is always fear. A couple of helpful slogans to me are "follow the fear" or "fear is a sign of growth".
— **Gloria Steinem**

I will do it scared when I am afraid.
I am up for the fight.
I am brave.
I can't be stopped…won't be shamed.
I am the power that creates change.

#100WaysToLoveYourself #BelieveBecomeRepeat

You can create the life you desire by concentrating on what you wish to attract. Once you master the idea surrounding this concept, you wont want to use your mind for the purpose of excuse making. Instead, youll prefer to use it to really consider what you want to manifest into your life and then visualize it as coming true.

– Wayne Dyer

I now release all physical, emotional, spiritual and any and all blockages, unknown and known from my body, mind, spirit and soul that has hindered me from becoming my best self. My energy is vibrant, loved filled and well positioned to only attract like energies.

Doubt, fear and negativity are not welcome inside of my heart, mind, spirit or body. I am in full control of all that is me and I am so thankful for who I am and who I am becoming.
I am limitless and a magnet for abundance. That abundance will allow me to be a wellspring for those in need.
I will call things that are not as if they are, until they are.

I will always live by my purpose and lead with love.
The love from my energy field will radiate before me, changing the atmosphere with his vibration.
I deserve the best, and that is exactly what I have.

I believe it, and it is so!

#100WaysToLoveYourself #BelieveBecomeRepeat

"Self-esteem
means
knowing you are
the dream."[31]
– Oprah Winfrey

I am in love with myself. There is no
part of my physical or spiritual being
that is not deserving of the deepest,
purest, honest, reciprocal love.
I am worthy of my own self-
love and will shower myself in it
daily regardless of anyone else's
feelings, actions, or lack thereof.
I am more than enough, and
was created for greatness!
I am a joy to be around, authentic,
righteous, faithful, honest, reliable, good-
natured, and every partner in my life will
mirror all of my amazing attributes.
Self-love is a requirement for anyone that
is already in or coming into my life.
I release every blockage that has
stood between me and what is
rightfully flowing to me.
I believe it, and it is so!

GEMS & STONES

1. Gems & Stones. I collect nuggets of knowledge and wisdom every chance that I get. Some people collect shot glasses, but I collect quotes, advice, song lyrics, life lessons, experiences, silly jokes, and animal videos. I have written and rewritten this section a few times because I want it to resonate with you, and for you to walk away with a beautiful gem in your pocket that you can pull out and admire later, or a cornerstone in life, upon which you can stand.

Everything isn't necessarily centered on self. In fact, there are a few gems like *Breaking Someone Else's Fall* or *Dating Up (Number 3 and 4 of this section)*, which both require interaction with someone else for it to work, but when you come across instances such as these, I hope that you are better prepared and can effectively navigate everything that will come your way. The stones that I hope you always stand on are practicing kindness until you are nearly perfect at it and talking to a therapist, counselor or other mental health professional may be what's needed to get your mental health in order. It's my belief that **we become rich mostly by the beauty and resilience that we carry in our hearts and souls**, and I hope that each of you reading this are certain of that after reading this book and that you spread your own gems & stones all over the world.

2. SURPRISE YOURSELF. One of my best friends had been single for a while before he decided that he was going to move from East Bumblephunk Nowhere to the city, with one purpose in mind: to find his wife. He got an apartment in the artsy part of town with all of the bells and whistles, but he still had a hard time meeting women. Then he signed up for *Match.com*. I was skeptical but kept it to myself. I just sort of went with it and matched his optimism, but my expectations were extremely low— especially when he started to actually date the girls. Not only were they unable to keep his attention, they were mostly nothing like who they presented themselves to be in their profiles (shocker), but as his friends, we were all hopeful. One day he mentioned that he was going out on a date with a girl from Oakland (and I, of course, was juiced), but I had no other feelings about it. I just wanted him to date someone as awesome as he is. The next morning after his date with "the girl from Oakland," he called me to say that it went extremely well. I was hopeful, but still not sold on the whole online dating thing until I met her. Immediately, I knew that he had been matched with his soulmate. Their energies and spirits were in alignment, and I knew that I was watching two people fall deeply in love every time I was around them. I named this section "Surprise Yourself" because that's exactly what he did, and he hit the jackpot. He wasn't the kind of person that would find love online. He is an outdoorsman who believes in getting his hands dirty, but **when you want something bad enough, you will try new ways of getting to it.** Three years later, I was among a small group of friends who awaited the two of them at a beautiful restaurant nestled in the Topanga Mountains when he proposed. A year after that I stood alongside him as a grooms-lady in one of the sweetest and most meaningful weddings that I have ever witnessed. Just yesterday, he was out of town, but his wife (and now my sister-friend) and their adorable daughter (my niece) were here for dinner and I just can't imagine my life without them. He surprised himself by taking this huge jump and had the most beautiful landing ever. Moreover, if he didn't love himself, he could not have attracted this mighty force of a wife who loves him deeply, but fiercely and unapologetically loves herself as well.

3. BREAK SOMEONE'S FALL. Every time I think of how much hurt I could have avoided had I only listened to people who had already walked miles in my shoes, I could just kick myself. I mean, obviously some lessons are learned best first-hand, but even then, if we listen to one another more, we could hear the stories of the formerly broken who, by the grace of God, have learned to put themselves back together again. The other part of this is that people that have made it out of horrifying experiences should share with others headed in the same direction in hopes to *break their fall*. We are all going to fall at some point, but some falls are harder to recover from than others. If I see someone who is about to date, or currently dating, someone who shows all of the signs of being abusive, I warn them. I don't wait for confirmation, I just preface it by saying, "I could be wrong, but…" If you find yourself in that position and would like to offer a little nudge in the right direction to someone headed for the danger zone, be sure to expect a little resistance because they will most likely fiercely defend this person that they barely know. Your job is to continue to be a friend and to look out for situations that threaten their safety. It's also your job to grab the beer or wine when they finally realized that you were right all along.

4. RELINQUISH CONTROL FROM YOUR YOUNGER SELF.

In my last book, there was a section where I wrote about having a conversation with your younger self, and that's important, but if you are anything like me, much of the pain that you have endured over the years is directly connected to the choices you made when you were younger. There is no sense in beating yourself up about that or obsessing over how things would or could have been had you done them differently. Even still, I highly recommend sitting down with that teenager or twenty-something boy or girl that is still in there somewhere and let them know that an adult is now in control. I realized how much I allowed things to stay the same while knee-deep in my own healing. In that soil where I was planted, I found so many ridiculous theories, rules and, quite frankly, things that have just gotten in my way. By now you know that I am big on visualizations, so I pictured myself in the car with my younger self; the self who thought that she was fat when she wasn't; the self who cried for days when a boy broke her heart; the self who barely required anything at all from someone who wanted her all. So, I sat in the car with her. The old VW bug that was given to us by Mother, and I snatched the keys. She fought because she was a spitfire, but

I am now an empowered woman who loves herself and there is no way that she is getting those keys back. I am now in control, leaving her in the past where she belongs, only resurfacing to gush about beautiful memories, but no more do I allow remnants of her horrible choices to govern my life. This may sound harsh to some, but tough love is necessary sometimes, especially when it comes to yourself.

5. PRACTICE KINDNESS. Kindness is natural for many, but it takes practice for most. If you are not sure if you're truly a kind person, ask someone you trust to share their honest opinion—, but be ready to receive constructive criticism! I could have named this *Call to Action* 'Be Kind', but so many of us need practice with it, and we cannot *be* anything that we just aren't. Growing up, people always asked me, "What's wrong?" Nothing was wrong most of the time, they were just reading into my facial expression, which wasn't always inviting. Since then, I have made it a practice to smile at passersby and to fix my face when I can catch myself looking upset or uninviting. I talked a bit about smiling early on in this book, but this digs a little deeper. Smiling isn't necessarily the basis of kindness, but it certainly is a universal and wordless language that is synonymous with being welcoming, happy and kind. The steps to practicing kindness require a bit more thought, consistency, and patience, but if you're not already doing the following, now is a great time to start:

- Volunteer
- Apologize
- Forgive
- Perform random acts of kindness

There are tons of other things that you can do, but this is the core group of actions that help me to stay grounded. It's so easy to get lost in our own world and become selfish, but self-love is not selfish, and it's not limited to just your core group of family and friends. **You are really showing that you love yourself when you can do something kind for others that is not meant to benefit you at all.** Volunteering and donating time are rites of passage for self-love. That song lyric, "what the world needs now is love sweet love. / It's the only thing that there's just too little of,"[32] is the truth. If we want love and kindness to circulate, we each have to do our part to put it out into the atmosphere.

Apologies and forgiveness are also important. So many people are spreading messages of love and manifestation all around the world, yet they have a long list of people who they have hurt right in their backyards. It is crucial to make amends and set those relationships right or stand the chance of that dust blowing right back into your own eyes. Simple apologies can repair gaping holes in sinking friendships.

Lastly, random acts of kindness. Do them. See how good it makes you feel to walk a neighbor's dog, deliver groceries to the elderly, mentor a child or even being kind to someone that you've been mean to for years prior. In the grand scheme of things, simple acts of kindness like these make the world a better place.

6. **WELCOME SIGNS!** - I am on a flight writing in my note app. What you're reading is copy-and-pasted into this book. I ran into my friend Allan Rich. He is a phenomenal songwriter, and through our very dear mutual friend Carol Ware, we have become great friends. Every time I see him it's like a gift from God that is sent to lift me. I was just crying on this plane. Acknowledging to God that I know good things are ahead. I talk to myself that way especially when I am UNcertain…it happens to all of us! And almost always I run into someone who drops huge gems into my soul. Today it was Allan. First off, I am on a plane from Fort Lauderdale to LA. I'm walking to my seat and see him. This makes me extremely happy. Then just like clockwork the woman next to me starts coughing. Not like coughing, coughing but like a serious wet splattering super contagious coughing! I take it as an opportunity to sanitize and stretch my legs instead of getting upset over something that I have absolutely no control of. I go to the restroom and see Allan again. Deciding to give the woman a moment alone, I talk to Allan and he filled me with everything that I needed. He said many things but one that resonates most was:

"Taura, you have rare air." He said that my aura was specific, and he spoke of how he constantly sees me manifesting greatness for myself. That was important because so often we don't see our good. We don't see our value. We just see our pain, struggles and fear but through his beautiful lens, I saw myself differently in a moment that I needed it most. And Allan is a songwriter... that is why this is even more special to me. God didn't have me run into a chef or dancer that I adore, he aligned my path with this beautiful soul who too was nominated for an Oscar and Golden Globe (twice). I'm almost sure that we are the only two people that shares that experience on this aircraft. Allan and his co-writer wrote, "Run to You" for Whitney Houston and "I Don't Have the Heart" for James Ingram, a beautiful soul that we recently lost. Allan shared a story about their hit song, "I Don't Have the Heart," and said that the label didn't want to release a third single, so they financed it themselves mostly because JAMES said, "Allan, we have to have faith." After it became a number one pop song, James called Allan to reinforce that sentiment of faith. He gushed about his experiences with James and my late musical father Leon Ware, as I struggled to listen over the roaring engines, and in that moment, I knew that we were sharing a moment ordered by the divine. Moments like these are signs that I welcome with the fullness of my being. Believe me, if you don't welcome them, you likely won't receive them. The Universe isn't wasting its time trying to convince people to believe. It instead connects with those who are wide open and welcoming the signs that it sends our way. On this particular day, I was in need of an encouraging word. Thank you Allan for being the vessel through which I saw my own greatness, again.

7. BREATHE. If you're feeling the least bit overwhelmed, then step away. Take a step back and think about the least stressful way for you to deal with any given situation. Even with this book, there is so much information, and you don't have to take it all in now if you feel you can't. **The biggest part of self-love is prioritizing ourselves and listening to our bodies. If you are feeling anxious or overwhelmed, breathing exercises can center you.** I particularly love this one from the *VeryWellMind.com*, "Simple Abdominal Breathing Exercise for Relaxation":

The next time you're feeling anxious try this simple relaxation technique:

1. *Inhale slowly and deeply through your nose. Keep your shoulders relaxed. Your abdomen should expand, and your chest should rise very little.*
2. *Exhale slowly through your mouth. As you blow air out, purse your lips slightly, but keep your jaw relaxed. You may hear a soft "whooshing" sound as you exhale.*
3. *Repeat this breathing exercise for several minutes.*

   You can perform this exercise as often as needed. It can be done standing up, sitting down, or lying down.

   If you find this exercise difficult or believe it's making you anxious or panicky, stop for now.[33]

8. Talk to Someone. Counseling was imperative for me both during and after my former marriage. I am so thankful for Pastor Andrea Humphrey for helping me in ways that she probably doesn't even know. I never once felt judged or that I could not tell her everything because she was my pastor—and that is a key component to finding the best person for you. You should be able to share your deepest darkest secrets and walk away feeling that they are safe with that person. According to *GoodTherapy.com*, "one in every five American adults has a mental condition, and people in talk-therapy explore their moods and behaviors in a safe place,"[34] and I couldn't agree more. I have a friend who is much better at being consistent with therapy than I am, and it shows. She is the friend I call when things are seemingly falling apart and she always knows how to talk me off the ledge, and I am so grateful to have her.

Writing this book has reminded me of so many of the things that I personally fall out of practice of. And while that's okay because I am human and I make mistakes, my greatest hope is that I learn from them all. I started this *Call to Action* by searching for a new therapist and thought to be as open and honest with you as possible. **No one has it all together, and that's okay**. The important thing is the effort that we each put into growing and learning. There are all kinds of therapy that target specific areas in life, including but not limited to depression, anxiety, compulsive disorders, phobias, restlessness, relationships, and just about anything else that you may be personally struggling with. What you may not know is that it does not cost a fortune and may be available with your health plan, or even provided for free by different organizations in your state or city. Therapy has been a touchy subject in the black community for years, but it's my hope that we release any negative thoughts about its efficacy back into the wild from which it came and embrace the collective need to heal. **We must take care of our entire selves and release the stigma associated with seeking mental wellness**. Thankfully, there are countless resources out there, and you may need to do a little research yourself locally, but below are several credible and reliable sources that I am hoping will land you in front of a therapist, and ultimately on the path of excellent mental health.

Therapyforblackgirls.com

Therapyforblackmen.org

Abpsi.org/find-psychologists/

Blog.zencare.co/how-to-find-a-black-therapist/

Eachmindmatters.org/mental-health/
diverse-communities/african-american/

Therapyforlatinx.com

Remezcla.com/lists/culture/mental-health-journey-latinos/

Wearemitu.com/things-that-matter/
therapy-latinx-mental-health-therapist-database/

9. **Date Up**. I have always been the kind of girl who dated down, and I have paid dearly for it. I don't know what it was, but I was only attracted to the bad boys in school, but they also had to be smart. Fast-forward to adulthood, and I finally grew up and accepted the idea that hanging on the street corner was not a viable career path, so I started to fall for another kind of guy... drum roll... THE MUSICIAN! I soon learned that most musicians are just bad boys with talent and huge egos. I ignored my mom, who told me that the nerd sitting at the front of the class would be the hot guy and most of the bad boys would be washed up. She was right. So many of the bad boys from high school still drink like we're at a keg party, except now their formerly adorable faces are filled with the wear-and-tear from years of drinking and partying. If I could go back to middle school and simply date up, I would have saved myself years of heartache and disappointment. It took me a few extremely hard falls to realize that dating the bad boy was actually due to my own poor self-image. Somewhere deep down I didn't realize that I didn't value myself enough. I didn't want the nerd in the front row because I didn't think that he would want me! Tapping into my "why" for dating the bad boy helped me to kiss goodbye the young lady inside of me who liked crying to sad songs on her pillow, and say hello to the woman who refuses anyone that is bad, rotten, or spoiled.

I started to have a more wholesome experience with dating only when I made myself accessible to guys who are respectful, hardworking, and GOOD MEN! I call it dating up, not necessarily because of the quality of guys, but because of myself. Dating up requires your potential partner or mate to at least meet you at eye-level. I spent so much time with my eyes staring at the ground or closed in tears that I wasn't looking up, wising up, or dating up until I realized the importance of my worth. This advice isn't reserved only for women. There are men who perpetually date bad girls as well, and if that's you, you need to *date pp* too, bro.

The first step to *dating up* is your mindset. And, believe me, it takes a lot of work to remove the thoughts that make us accept less than what we deserve. I went to counseling to deal with those things and eventually started valuing the advice I was given. You could be 16 or 61, it's never too late.

I thought that this would be a good opportunity to compare your dream partner with your reality partner (can be the last person that you dated). The only rule here is to be completely honest with yourself. When you complete each question, write a statement about both the dream-person and the reality-person. Things are a bit clearer when in black and white. Your dream-person assessment may be that you have yet to meet, based on the questions, or it may help you to realize that the reality and dream person are one and the same. However, what's equally important is to hold yourself under the same scrutiny, because you can't expect someone to have all of these things if you don't. **Be very honest and vulnerable in your own personal assessment of yourself.**

QUALITIES	DREAM PERSON	REALITY PERSON
Is he/she honest?	☐	☐
Is he/she reliable?	☐	☐
Is he/she secure?	☐	☐
Is he/she even tempered?	☐	☐
Is he she practical?	☐	☐
Is he/she a good listener?	☐	☐
Is this person consistent?	☐	☐
Is this person good with money?	☐	☐
Does this person live on his/her own?	☐	☐
Does he/she have sustainable employment?	☐	☐
Are you in agreement with core values/life goals?	☐	☐
Are you able to be yourself with this person?	☐	☐
Is this person malicious or violent?	☐	☐
Does this person hide important details?	☐	☐
Has this person cheated on you?	☐	☐
Does your intuition give you any alarms about this person?	☐	☐
Is this person an optimist?	☐	☐
Do you feel safe with this person?	☐	☐
Does this person make you a priority?	☐	☐
Does this person encourage you?	☐	☐
Do you balance one another?	☐	☐
Does this person love him/herself?	☐	☐

#100WaysToLoveYourself #BelieveBecomeRepeat

Now circle the above attributes that relate to you. Are you all of the things that you desire in someone else.

10. **END THE WAR OF WORDS. What we say to each other is changing the landscape of the world.** Kids are actually committing suicide because other kids are ripping them to shreds with their sharp tongues. It's hard to stop because it's coming from the top of the food chain. I am embarrassed as an American when I see our current president bullying, demeaning, and degrading others on social media and in the press, but all that I can control is my own tongue and the same goes for you. The world is a different place and we must act accordingly, such as learning to use our voices in ways that best serve everyone and to fight for social justice reform and support diversity and inclusion; but raising our voices without raising awareness for something or someone in need, is just noise.

RECIPES FOR SELF-CARE

I was raised by a very creative woman, my beautiful mother, Yvonne Stinson. To this very day, she can give you a recipe for just about anything, from beauty products to food, and it looks like I developed the same creative gene! My best friend Kyra and I used to sleep in mayonnaise and olive oil hair treatments long before there were Olive Oil & Mayonnaise treatments. Although we hated smelling like sandwiches and having oil run down our necks, when the pressing comb was put against our hair, it glided like silk. Over the years, I have followed in my mom's footsteps, and make everything from scrubs and conditioners to tonics and scalp treatments. The next ten recipes are some of the ones I use on Self-Care Sunday, but you can whip these up seven days a week. For me, Sunday is the day when I usually go to church or spend one-on-one time with the Creator, and when that's over, I am at home treating myself to inexpensive but decadent and relaxing treatments. Keep in mind that self-care isn't reserved only for women. The epidermis is the biggest organ, and it needs to be moisturized, exfoliated and protected from the sun regardless of gender. Do it together with a group of friends, or alone. Your body will thank you!

believebecomerepeat

Sea Salt & Sugar Scrub

½ cup coarse sea salt
¼ cup of coconut oil
5 drops of Eucalyptus essential oil

½ cup raw sugar
2 tablespoons of dried lavender flower
5 drops of tea tree oil

Directions:
This is a coarse body scrub. The only things that may need to be ground in your bullet or similar device are the lavender flowers. They should be a powdery consistency. Stir all of the ingredients together and store in a cool dry place.

Benefits:
The magnesium in salt is great for the skin, but I find salt alone too harsh, so I always add sugar to it. According to OrganicFacts.com, coconut oil is beneficial in aiding various ailments including Eczema & Psoriasis and Dermatitis.

#100WaysToLoveYourself #BelieveBecomeRepeat

Directions: This is a coarse body scrub. The only things that may need to be ground in your Bullet (or similar blending device) are the lavender flowers. They should be a powdery consistency. Stir all the ingredients together and store in a cool dry place.

Benefits: The magnesium in salt is great for the skin, but I find that salt alone is too harsh, so I always add sugar to it. According to *OrganicFacts.com*, coconut oil is beneficial in aiding various ailments including Eczema & Psoriasis and Dermatitis.[35]

believebecomerepeat

Red Rice Water Treatment

1 cup of uncooked Rice
100 % pure cranberry juice

1 cup of distilled water
10 drops of clary sage

Directions:
After rinsing and draining the rice, place it into a glass container and pour water over it. Allow it to ferment for 12 hours. Drain into a cup with a spout, like a measuring cup. Pour rice water into a spray bottle and add cranberry juice, clary sage and shake vigorously. Place a towel over your neck and shoulders and saturate freshly washed hair in the Red Rice Water. Do not dry. Place a plastic cap over your hair and allow it to sit for no more than two hours. Rinse thoroughly and refrigerate unused portion for up to 7 days.

Benefits:
The magnesium in salt is great for the skin, but I find salt alone too harsh, so I always add sugar to it. According to OrganicFacts.com, coconut oil is beneficial in aiding various ailments including Eczema & Psoriasis and Dermatitis.

#100WaysToLoveYourself #BelieveBecomeRepeat

Directions: After rinsing and draining the rice, place it into a glass container and pour water over it. Allow it to ferment for 12 hours. Drain into a cup with a spout, (like a measuring cup). Pour rice water into a spray bottle and add cranberry juice, clary sage and shake vigorously. Place a towel over your neck and shoulders and saturate freshly washed hair in the Red Rice Water. Do not dry. Place a plastic cap over your hair and allow it to sit for no more than two hours. Rinse thoroughly and refrigerate unused portion for up to 7 days.

SideBar: You will smell like Thanksgiving, but your hair will be the one thanking you. Also, if you have light-colored hair, use white 100% organic white cranberry juice or juice white cranberries. Do not leave this treatment on overnight. It may deposit too much protein and cause hair breakage.

Benefits: Per *Essence.com*, rice water stimulates hair growth and repairs dry hair, among other amazing benefits.[36] Cranberries are anti-inflammatory **and are great for the scalp, as is clary sage which blocks and overproduction of sebum.**

believebecomerepeat

Mama's Mayo Treatment Mask

1 egg yolk
1/3 Cup of Organic Mayo
Two tablespoons Organic Olive Oil
1 tsp sweet almond oil

Directions:
Whip the egg yolk in your Bullet or small blender. Slowly add all ingredients. Use a pre wash treatment. Leave on from 15 minutes – Overnight. Wash and style prior to rinsing out. Refrigerate for up to 48 hours. Discard thereafter.

Benefits:
Egg Yolks – Prevent breakage, Mayo – Improves texture, Olive Oil – Hydrates & Fights dandruff, sweet almond oil – protects skin from UV radiation.

#100WaysToLoveYourself #BelieveBecomeRepeat

Directions: Whip the egg yolk in your Bullet or small blender. Slowly add all ingredients. Use as a pre-wash treatment. Leave on anywhere for 15 minutes - overnight. Wash after initial rinse. Refrigerate for up to 48 hours. Discard thereafter.

Benefits: Egg Yolks prevent breakage; Mayo improves texture; Olive Oil hydrates & fights dandruff; and Sweet Almond Oil protects skin from UV radiation.

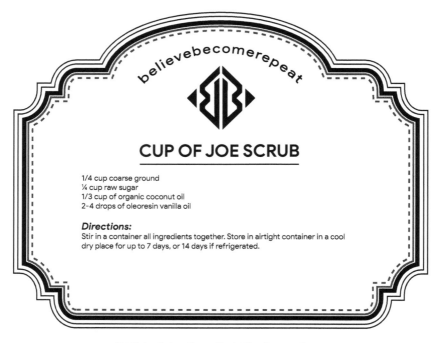

believebecomerepeat

CUP OF JOE SCRUB

1/4 cup coarse ground
¼ cup raw sugar
1/3 cup of organic coconut oil
2-4 drops of oleoresin vanilla oil

Directions:
Stir in a container all ingredients together. Store in airtight container in a cool dry place for up to 7 days, or 14 days if refrigerated.

#100WaysToLoveYourself #BelieveBecomeRepeat

Directions: Stir in a container all ingredients together. Store in an airtight container in a cool dry place for up to 7 days, or 14 days if refrigerated.

believebecomerepeat

SPA FACIAL SCRUB

¼ cup of coarse sugar
¼ cup vitamin e oil
1 drop of tea tree essential oil
1 drop of rosemary essential oil

Directions:
Mix all ingredients together by hand. Store in airtight container in a cool dry place for up to 14 days.

Benefits:
Raw Sugar; Natural exfoliant, Vitamin E Oil – Skin Cancer prevention, Tea tree Oil – Antifungal, rosemary oil –antimicrobial

#100WaysToLoveYourself #BelieveBecomeRepeat

Directions; Mix all ingredients together by hand. Store in an airtight container in a cool dry place for up to 14 days.

Benefits: Raw Sugar is a natural exfoliant; Vitamin E Oil helps prevent Skin Cancer; Tea Tree Oil is antifungal; and rosemary oil is antimicrobial.

believebecomerepeat

MINT & ROSE SKIN TOINC

½ cup organic dried rose petals
¼ cup fresh mint leaves
2 cups distilled water
2 drops of tea tree essential oil

Directions:
Place dried rose petals in water and bring to a boil. Reduce and simmer on low for about five minutes. Cool down, add fresh mint and pour into a glass container with a tight cover like a mason jar. Set aside overnight. Strain mint and roses and pour into a spray bottle. Top with two drops of tea tree oil. Keeps for about a month if refrigerated. Use to tone, prep and refresh.

Benefits:
Mint- Hydrates/Brightens

#100WaysToLoveYourself #BelieveBecomeRepeat

Directions: Place dried rose petals in water and bring to a boil. Reduce and simmer on low for about five minutes. Cool down, add fresh mint, and pour into a glass container with a tight cover (like a mason jar). Set aside overnight. Strain mint and roses and pour into a spray bottle. Top with two drops of tea tree oil. Keeps for about a month if refrigerated. Use to tone, prep, and refresh.

Benefits: Mint hydrates and brightens.

believebecomerepeat

SCALP SAVIOR

1 ounce of Castor Oil
4 drops of Apple cider vinegar
2 drops of clary sage essential oil
2 drops tea tree oil

1-ounce vitamin E oil
6 drops of Frankincense
2 drops rosemary essential oil

Directions:
Fill 4-ouncie glass dropper with all ingredients. Store in a cool dry place. Use in troubled spots before bed.

Benefits:
Castor oil – Growth, Vitamin E Oil – Moisturizes (see above for other benefits)

#100WaysToLoveYourself #BelieveBecomeRepeat

Directions: Fill a 4-ounce glass dropper with all ingredients. Store in a cool dry place. Use in troubled spots before going to bed.

Benefits: Castor oil promotes hair growth; Vitamin E Oil moisturizes.

believebecomerepeat

BEARD BUTTER

1/3-cup cocoa butter
¼ cup coconut oil
3 drops peppermint oil
3 drops lavender oil
Avocado oil

Directions:
Whip cocoa butter and coconut oil until smooth. Transfer to a container with a tight
top and drop in essential oils. Emulsify and use as a balm or pack on and allow it to
sit for 5 minutes to use as a conditioner.

#100WaysToLoveYourself #BelieveBecomeRepeat

Directions: Whip cocoa butter and coconut oil until smooth. Transfer to a container with a tight top and drop in essential oils. Emulsify and use as a balm or pack on and allow it to sit for 5 minutes to use as a conditioner.

believebecomerepeat

Not Your Store Bought Braid Spray

3 ounces Mint & Rose Skin Tonic (recipe above)
3 ounces of grape seed oil
3 ounces coconut water
4 drops clary sage oil
4 drops thyme oil

3 ounces aloe juice
4 drops of tea tree oil
4 drops rosemary oil

Directions:
follow instructions above to make the rose & mint skin tonic. Add all ingredients into a quality 12 ounce spray bottle and shake. Store in a cook, dry place. Keeps for about 2 months.

#100WaysToLoveYourself #BelieveBecomeRepeat

Directions: follow the instructions above to make the rose & mint skin tonic. Add all ingredients into a quality 12-ounce spray bottle and shake. Store in a cool, dry place. Keeps for about 2 months.

believebecomerepeat

MIMOSA CLAY MASK

½ cup dry champagne
1-cup clay
1 tsp honey
2-3 drops of essential oil

Directions:
This is my go to mask for girls night. You can make it fund by
setting up stations for each of your guests with sharpies, labels and empty
containers. In addition you can make your own bars of add ones with various
essential oils, and ingredients like turmeric, chopped strawberries, green
vegetable powder and blue-green algae to make fun colors with varying
benefits.

#100WaysToLoveYourself #BelieveBecomeRepeat

Directions: This is my go-to mask for a girls' night. You can make it fun by setting up stations for each of your guests with sharpies, labels, and empty containers. In addition, you can make your own bars of add-ons with various essential oils, and ingredients like turmeric, chopped strawberries, green vegetable powder, and blue-green algae to make fun colors with varying benefits.

NO MORE...

Say "no more" before each of these actions...

1. **Self-Doubt!** Self-doubt takes only but a moment to set in, so be vigilant about guarding your thoughts, the company that you keep and what you allow into your space. Everything from music to podcasts can be emotionally and spiritually crippling, but the most successful cultivators and planters of the self-doubt seeds are the people we love. Some of them mean well, but some don't. You have to find the courage to disconnect yourself completely from the ladder and let those who mean well know how their negativity is affecting your progress. Don't spend too much time talking about it. This is your life and that conversation (should you feel it necessary to have) is a courtesy to them. Your life is not meant to be spent doubting your dreams and abilities, so when a wave of doubt starts to rise against you, you must be armed and prepared to win this war against yourself. Here are some ideas (some of this will sound familiar):

"Comparison is the thief of joy!"
– Unknown

✓ Limit social media usage
✓ Practice self-affirmations
✓ Limit time with pessimists
✓ Increase time with optimists
✓ Count your blessings
✓ Go on a television fast
✓ Honor your accomplishments
✓ Read an inspiring book
✓ Trust Yourself
✓ Admire his/her beauty/accomplishments /life without questioning your own.

#100WaysToLoveYourself #BelieveBecomeRepeat

2. Substance & Alcohol Abuse! Get help. Tomorrow is not promised for anyone, but if you are struggling or have a problem with substance and alcohol abuse, you need support. The government has a resource available for called SAMHSA. The acronym stands for Substance Abuse and Mental Health Services. According to their website,[37] they are open 24/7 and will connect you with the appropriate local source.

The national helpline for SAMHSA is 1-800-662-HELP (4357).

3. **NEGATIVE SELF-TALK!** Encourage yourself to do your best, of course, but no more bashing yourself. I know this first hand because I used to do it almost every day. **If you don't believe you are beautiful, stand in the mirror and say it to yourself until you believe it!** Talk to yourself the way you would a friend that you really

care about. Nurture the seeds of dreams inside of you, instead of hitting them with the weed-whacker! Remember that wildflowers grow from those very weeds. Find the beauty and value that it is right inside of you. At any given time, you can catch me on the highway audibly flipping negative thoughts on their backs and smothering them with a positive thought. If something rises up in me and says, "you are ugly," I say the total opposite until the original thought disappears. All of this is a lot of work, but it's your life. Who else is going to do it?

4. PUTTING MYSELF ON HOLD! Parents, this is for you especially. If you want to be there for your children, schedule your annual checkup on the same day that they have there's. Meal prep for yourself when you are making their lunches. Go back and get your degree and do whatever it is that sets your soul on fire. The same goes for you workaholics and students. Don't let life live you, embrace it while there is still air in your lungs. Say yes to something. Try a new food. Be bold and daring. Fall in love with yourself so fiercely that others have no choice but to do the same.

5. ABUSE OF ANY KIND! Emotional, verbal, physical, workplace, financial, spiritual, or whatever else is beating you up <u>has to go</u>! You were not made to be anyone's punching bag and you have the same rights to happiness as your perpetrator. Stand up for yourself before you wake up and it's ten years later and you are in the same bondage. If you are in a physically abusive relationship, there are steps that need to be taken to ensure your safety. I have been there, and by the grace of God, I am free, thriving and no longer under the thumb of fear. What you have to know, 100%, is that the horrible things you see on the news or read in the paper can happen to you if you do not get the hell out of there. *HelpGuide.Org* has some really smart advice that you may find useful. For some of you, there will not be time to visit a website and call help centers. My advice to you is not to believe a single word that your abusers say and to get out the first chance that you get. Be well aware that your phone/computer security may be compromised, so be careful and strategic. You can

149

also call the National Domestic Violence hotline. They will connect you with local sources. Their number is 800-799-7233, but if you are in a life-threatening situation, find a way to call 911. Another thing to do is consider making a safe-word and share it with one of your children, neighbors or someone that may routinely hear the violence happening. The most important thing for you to remember is that it will more than likely happen again. I don't want you to be another hashtag or news story. Be a phoenix that rises from the ashes and flies with brave wings. Sending love, light, healing, and protective energy to anyone reading this that does not feel safe. Please talk to someone.

6. **GIVING UP ON MY DREAMS!** Dreams only die when we do not keep them alive. You are the breath in your dream's lungs, and it needs you for its survival. I can't live your dreams for you. Your spouse can't live your dreams. Your kids can't live your dreams. Only you can. It takes hard work most of the time, but that's okay. You will become more invigorated when you see the little buds start to sprout from your growing dream. Then you'll water and feed it and then work some more. The next time you come back around you'll see the branches start to form, and then finally you will be able to taste the fruit of your dreams. It's a part of what life is about. You were born with a purpose! Connect that purpose to your dreams and put it into action and see how you feel. I know the bills are stacked high, and the morale is low, but we have control over the ladder. Think your dreams are true. It is more than possible; people are manifesting their dreams every day with less than you. Below is a starter kit. It's loosely based on what I wrote for myself years ago when I decided not to take the job that would have paid me beautifully to cultivate someone else's dream. I am so grateful that I took that chance on myself, and it won't be the last time. I am continuously watering the dreams planted in my mind.

(Please use the spaces beneath each question or suggestion for answers, thoughts and plans.)

1. What are you dreams? (Name at least two)

_____

_____

_____

2. What steps have you taken to make one or all of them come true?

_____

_____

_____

3. Name three people that you are not connected to that are living your dream. (Feel free to Google them)

_____

_____

_____

4. What are they doing that you did not do?

_____

_____

_____

5. Name three people that have similar paths, even if in a different field that you are connected to.

_____

_____

_____

6. Draft and email to each of them requesting a meeting or call. If they are not available, pull from people that you do not know and request a meeting.

_____

_____

_____

(Please use the spaces beneath each question or suggestion for answers, thoughts and plans.)

7. Start to formulate a plan by making a list of actions and goals.

_____

_____

_____

8. Be sure to be 100% certain of your plan before sharing with anyone that is personally connected to you.

_____

_____

_____

9. Enlist the help of a professional or app to write an effective business plan.

_____

_____

_____

10. Write it. (your business plan)

_____

_____

_____

11. Make a list of three things that you can do now that is either on the list or in your plan.

_____

_____

_____

12. Do them.

_____

_____

_____

(Please use the spaces beneath each question or suggestion for answers, thoughts and plans.)

13. Study the industry that your dream is rooted in.

_____

_____

_____

14. Gain hands on knowledge (work in your desired industry part-time)

_____

_____

_____

15. Remind your self how this dream is tied to your purpose

_____

_____

_____

16. Manifest the right people into your life that can be instrumental in birthing this dream.

_____

_____

_____

17. Network with people already in the field.

_____

_____

18. Find a mentor.

_____

_____

_____

#100WaysToLoveYourself #BelieveBecomeRepeat

19. Accept support from people that love you.

_____

_____

_____

20. Jump.

_____

_____

_____

#100WaysToLoveYourself #BelieveBecomeRepeat

7. Spending Time with People Who Do Not Mean Well For Me! You know who they are, but you haven't let go because it hurts like hell to rip apart from someone you have known forever or someone you love deeply, but you've got to do it because those feelings rub off on you. That energy gets into your psyche and all of a sudden you wonder why you think you are not talented, worthy, beautiful, smart, or whatever else their negative asses are projecting onto you. There are plenty of people in this world filled with love. Manifest them into your life and ask God to reveal and remove those who are not filled with love. If you are on a quest to love yourself as deeply as you have loved others, then really take this to heart. I've said it in as many ways as I can because it is so important. I personally do not subscribe to the theory that one needs to be successful to be my friend. I think that's limiting and horrible, in fact, because then I would miss out on a few people in my life who have not yet figured out their careers or finances but are happy, whole, and righteous souls who I love dearly. The measure of a human is not his or her bank account, it's their capacity to love others and themselves. Those who truly love themselves will always want the best for you.

8. CUTTING MYSELF ON BROKEN PROMISES! If I had a cut for promises that I broke to myself, I would have bled out long ago. I changed this section to the first person because I am human, I'm not perfect and I have to scream these no-mores to myself too. I can find a million excuses to break my own promises, and yet I find a way to be 100% reliable to everyone else. Those days over. I am holding myself to those same standards and prioritizing me in ways that I haven't before. At the same time, I am also not allowing the promises of the ones I love to cut me either. I'm not here for people who routinely don't keep their word or are just unreliable. Me accepting that sends a message to them that I don't value myself, and I do, but my goal is to do so more fiercely, and I hope the same for you. I need to be able to walk barefoot through my own life unharmed, and that takes time, and I am admittedly not there yet. It's time to engage several of the rules that we started within this book. Get your brooms and let's go!

9. LIMITING THOUGHTS! I was the person who would say, "Look at her—she's so amazing. I could never do that." Then I developed this 'Believe-Become-Repeat' mindset, and I did those things exactly, like self-publishing my first book, getting the nominations and, more importantly, successfully navigating my own life on my own terms. Then Doubt's cousin, Self-Limiting Thoughts, comes for me and I admit that I have fallen for it a time or two. It says things like, "You can lose weight, but never that much." Or, "you can live by music but you're too old to write for some of the new artists or new mediums out there." At a different time, I would have let these thoughts govern my life, but now I use them as fuel to break through my own personal challenges. There is no limit to what I can do. I am a black woman who is plus-sized and over forty, but I am also a righteous soul, an Oscar/Golden Globe/Grammy nominee, co-chair of the diversity and inclusion initiative for the music branch at AMPAS, and an award-winning author and writer, and I just completed my first European tour in a job where the average woman is 19-32 years old, and I am not finished yet. I am thankful for this journey and hope that the strides that I make encourage you to break the self-imposed limits of your thoughts and be free to be 100% whatever you choose to be. Sometimes our environments dictate our paths so put headphones and blinders on if you have to. Meaning if you have a negative boo, parents, spouse, or whatever, block them out so that the limits they impose on you do not bleed onto this clear picture you have of yourself.

10. **SELF-HATRED**. Hate is a strong word, but it is not stronger than love.

Love is stronger than pride, fear, prejudice, racism, ageism, sexism, gender bias, boundaries, walls, injustices, circumstances, suicide, guns, bombs, lies, disease, poverty, wealth, politics, corruption, judgment, pain and everything under the sun except you; because love lives inside of you... you are one and the same. When you tap into your capacity to love your entire self, you will have the propensity to move mountains and become fluent in this universal language without even speaking one word. #NoteToSelf

"DO THE WORK" BOOK

John C. Maxwell struck a chord in millions, if not billions when he said, "Dreams don't work unless you do."[38] Reading that was like gospel for me because it is. James 2:26 in the Bible says, "faith without works is dead."[39] That's an extremely popular scripture, which I plant one foot on, while the other is planted on

I Corinthians 13:2
And if I have the gift of prophecy,
and know all mysteries and all
knowledge; and if I have all faith,
so as to remove mountains, but
have not love, I am nothing.[40]

This book was written on those two premises, doing the work and the complete and utter reverence of love—love for myself first, so that I have the capacity to love others; if I am jealous and at war with myself, then I will, undoubtedly, be the same with everyone else. I know that to be true because I have been there, and the process of peeling back those layers to get to where I am now has challenged and stretched me, but I am better for it, and I hope that you are too. I started off by writing about personal experiences that I hoped someone would read and would know that I was talking about them. I wanted them, if just for a moment, to hurt like me. But like Maya Angelou said to Oprah, "When you know better, you do better."[41] The thing about knowing is that there are levels to it. On the surface, I knew it wasn't the coolest thing to do, but it wasn't until I started to dig that I started to feel convicted by it and knew for sure that I had to change my approach. Needless to say, those sections ended up in the trash, where they belong. The experiences that made the final edit are pure, unpretentious and from my heart. I have learned firsthand that that is where self-love lives.

It's my genuine hope and prayer that everyone who reads this tap into the wellspring of self-love inside of them. Life teaches us to love others and to be good to people, and to respect them, but the message for self-love, self-respect, and self-esteem isn't as loud and clear. We, as women, are taught to shrink ourselves to make others feel more comfortable, submit to our husbands, shroud ourselves in secrecy, and to always be perfect. But that's not who we really are. We have opinions that are wide, bold, and spilling out of the boxes that were built for us hundreds, if not thousands of years ago, and we want out.

There are men who feel similarly or maybe even disconnected from the societal expectations of masculinity. These are some of the reasons people are walking around unhappy and unable to love themselves; because they don't even feel free to be themselves. Where there is no freedom, love is a hard concept to grasp.

And as we come to the end of this experience together, I hope that you have, at the very least, found a floating device that can carry you through the ocean of emotions and thoughts, safely to the banks of self-love.

The last ten *Calls to Action* will be your own. Please be as honest and gentle with yourself as possible.

1. Who do you need to forgive, and why?

_____

_____

_____

_____

_____

_____

_____

_____

_____

_____

_____

_____

_____

_____

_____

_____

_____

_____

_____

_____

_____

#100WaysToLoveYourself #BelieveBecomeRepeat

2. Do you love yourself? If so, explain what that means. If not then tell yourself why.

_____

_____

_____

_____

_____

_____

_____

_____

_____

_____

_____

_____

_____

_____

_____

_____

_____

_____

_____

_____

#100WaysToLoveYourself #BelieveBecomeRepeat

3. Who do you personally know that truly loves his or herself? What have your learned from them?

_____

_____

_____

_____

_____

_____

_____

_____

_____

_____

_____

_____

_____

_____

_____

_____

_____

_____

_____

_____

#100WaysToLoveYourself #BelieveBecomeRepeat

4. Are you where you want to be in life? If not, how will you get there?

_____

_____

_____

_____

_____

_____

_____

_____

_____

_____

_____

_____

_____

_____

_____

_____

_____

_____

_____

#100WaysToLoveYourself #BelieveBecomeRepeat

5. What areas of self-love need the most improvement in your life? Write from its perspective. For instance, if your body/ spirit/mind could talk what would it say?

_____

_____

_____

_____

_____

_____

_____

_____

_____

_____

_____

_____

_____

_____

_____

_____

_____

_____

#100WaysToLoveYourself #BelieveBecomeRepeat

6. Are you living your dreams? If so, how? If not, how?

#100WaysToLoveYourself #BelieveBecomeRepeat

7. Is there something or someone hindering you from fully loving yourself? If so, who/what/how?

8. Write three short letters of gratitude to your past, present and future self.

_____

_____

_____

_____

_____

_____

_____

_____

_____

_____

_____

_____

_____

_____

_____

_____

_____

_____

_____

_____

#100WaysToLoveYourself #BelieveBecomeRepeat

9. Write a list of goals that you have for yourself. They can be from any perspective (emotional, physical, spiritual, etc.) Your homework beyond the confines of these pages is to write plans of action for those things in a separate journal, and check them of as they are accomplished. (Make notes below)

10. Who are you? Not your name, but the essence of your being? And what is love?

_____

_____

_____

_____

_____

_____

_____

_____

_____

_____

_____

_____

_____

_____

_____

_____

_____

_____

_____

_____

#100WaysToLoveYourself #BelieveBecomeRepeat

One more thing.
Please draw your final self-portrait for this experience.

#BELIEVEBECOMEREPEAT #100WAYSTOLOVEYOURSELF

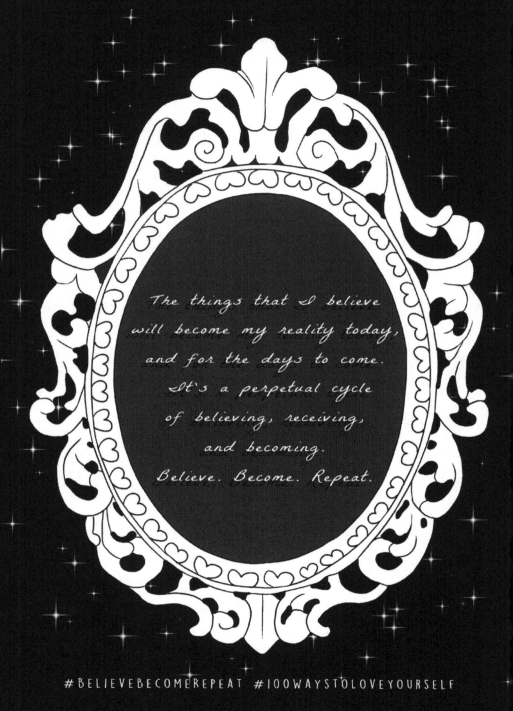

The things that I believe
will become my reality today,
and for the days to come.
It's a perpetual cycle
of believing, receiving,
and becoming.
Believe. Become. Repeat.

#BELIEVEBECOMEREPEAT #100WAYSTOLOVEYOURSELF

NOTES

1. Forest, Danny. "Becoming, Attracting And Creating, According to Buddha." *Medium*, September 13, 2019. https://medium.com/swlh/becoming-attracting-and-creating-according-to-buddha-49694643e5a.

2. Proverbs 23:7 (King James Version).

3. Badu, Erykah, "Bag Lady." 1998, Motown Records, track 12 on *Mama's Gun*, Released 2000, compact disc.

4. "Forgiveness: Your Health Depends on It." *Johns Hopkins Medicine*. Accessed October 15, 2019. https://www.hopkinsmedicine.org/health/wellness-and-prevention/forgiveness-your-health-depends-on-it.

5. Fox, David. "Forgiveness is the Fragrance the Violet Sheds on the Heel That Has Crushed it." *Fox Psychology*, July 4, 2018 https://foxpsychology.com.au/2018/07/04/forgiveness-is-the-fragrance-the-violet-sheds-on-the-heel-that-has-crushed-it-mark-twain/

6. "Before You Embark On a Journey…" *The Mind's Journal*, July 11, 2018, https://themindsjournal.com/before-you-embark-on-a-journey-of-revenge/

7. "Jalal Al-Din Rumi." *Poets.org*. Academy of American Poets. Retrieved from https://poets.org/poet/jalal-al-din-rumi.

8. Goldstein, Gloria, Ph.D. "Our Barriers to Love: Monday's Mindful Quote from Rumi." *Psych Central,* February 15, 2010, https://blogs.psychcentral.com/mindfulness/2010/02/our-barriers-to-love-mondays-mindful-quote-with-rumi/.

9. Badu, Erykah. "Bag Lady," 1998

10. Verghese, Joe, Richard B. Lipton, Mindy J. Katz, Charles B. Hall, Carol A. Derby, Gail Kuslansky, Anne F. Ambrose, Martin Sliwinski, and Herman Buschke. "Leisure Activities and the Risk of Dementia in the Elderly." *New England Journal of Medicine* 348, no. 25 (2003): 2508–16. https://doi.org/10.1056/nejmoa022252.

11. Powers, Richard, "Use It or Lose It: Dancing Makes You Smarter, Longer." *Stanford University*, 30 July 2010, https://socialdance.stanford.edu/syllabi/smarter.htm.

12. "What Happens When You Believe in Yourself - Steve Harvey Jump Motivational Speech," YouTube video, 0:33, "The Outcome," June 29, 2019, https://www.youtube.com/watch?v=kLojr1kpk5Y

13. Lane, Derrick, "Golden Medicine: How Gold Affects Your Body." BlackDoctor.org, 5 July 2018, https://blackdoctor.org/522429/golden-medicine-how-gold-affects-your-body/.

14. Worrall, Simon, "We Are Stardust-Literally." National Geographic, 28 Jan. 2015, www.nationalgeographic.com/news/2015/01/150128-big-bang-universe-supernova-astrophysics-health-space-ngbooktalk/.

15. Angelou, Maya, *I Know Why the Caged Bird Sings.* New York: Random House Trade Paperback, 2009

16. Hill, Lauryn, "Ex-Factor." recorded December 1997, Ruffhouse/Columbia Records, Track 3 on *The Miseducation of Lauryn Hill,* 1998, compact disc.

17. "Destination Healthy Aging: The Physical, Cognitive and Social Benefits of Travel." [Fact Sheet] Global Coalition on Aging, 2013.

18. "The Power of Positive Thinking." *Johns Hopkins Medicine.* Accessed October 15, 2019. https://www.hopkinsmedicine.org/health/healthy_aging/healthy_mind/the-power-of-positive-thinking?sponsor=252865.

19. Dellner, Alexia. "16 Quotes From Oprah Winfrey That Will Give You *Life*," *Pure Wow,* January 29, 2019, https://www.purewow.com/entertainment/oprah-quotes.

20. Van DeVenter, Judson W., "I Surrender All." Composed by Winfield S. Weedon, 1896, Sebring Publishing Co., *Gospel Songs of Grace and Glory.*

21. "Self-Affirmation." In *Merriam-Webster's Collegiate Dictionary.* Retrieved from https://www.merriam-webster.com/dictionary/self-affirmation.

22. King, Martin Luther. *A Testament of Hope: the Essential Writings and Speeches of Martin Luther King, Jr.* Edited by James Melvin Washington. New York: HarperOne, an imprint of HarperCollins Publishers, 2006.

23. Matt. 7:7 (KJV)

24. Jean-Philippe, McKenzie, "20 Timeless Toni Morrison Quotes That Will Always Stay With You," *The Oprah Magazine*, Aug 6, 2019. https://www.oprahmag.com/life/g28621944/toni-morrison-quotes/

25. Curry, Colleen. "Maya Angelou's Wisdom Distilled in 10 of Her Best Quotes," *ABC News*, May 28, 2014, https://abcnews.go.com/Entertainment/maya-angelous-wisdom-distilled-10-best-quotes/story?id=23895284.

26. Shange, Ntozake. *For Colored Girls Who Have Considered Suicide, When the Rainbow Is Enuf: a Choreopoem*, 92, New York, NY: Scribner, 2010.

27. Tolle, Eckhart. *A New Earth: Awakening to Your Life's Purpose*, 96, New York, NY: Plume, 2006.

28. Tolle. *A New Earth*, 190.

29. "We Are Shaped By Our Thoughts…" *Psychology Tomorrow Magazine*, June 24, 2016, http://psychologytomorrowmagazine.com/we-are-shaped-by-our-

thoughts-we-become-what-we-think-when-the-mind-is-pure-joy-follows-like-a-shadow-that-never-leaves-buddha/.

30. Dyer, Wayne. *Excuses Begone! How to Change a Lifetime of Self-Defeating Thinking Habits*, 100, Carlsbad, CA: Hay House, 2009

31. Juma, Norbert "Oprah Winfrey Quotes to inspire Passion, Leadership and Love." *Everyday Power,* April 16, 2018, https://everydaypower.com/oprah-winfrey-quotes-about-life/.

32. Bacharach, Burt and Hal David, *"What the World Needs Now is Love"*, with Jackie DeShannon, April 15, 1965, Imperial Records, 1965.

33. Ankrom, Sheryl, "How to Breathe Properly for Relieving Your Anxiety." *Verywell Mind*, 19 Sept. 2019, www.verywellmind.com/abdominal-breathing-2584115.

34. "Benefits of Psychotherapy." *GoodTherapy.com*, Good Therapy, 1 Aug. 2018, www.goodtherapy.org/benefits-of-therapy.html.

35. Nagdeve, Meenakshi. "16 Proven Health Benefits & Uses of Coconut Oil." *Organic Facts*, 19 Oct. 2019, www.organicfacts.net/health-benefits/oils/health-benefits-of-coconut-oil.html.

36. Wilson, Alexandra. "Natural Hair Growth Hack: Here's the Secret to Healthy Hair Using Rice Water." *Essence*, 5 Dec. 2018, www.essence.com/hair/natural-hair-growth-hack-heres-the-secret-to-healthy-hair-using-rice-water/.

37. "National Helpline." *SAMHSA*, U.S. Dept. of Health and Human Services, 25 Oct. 2019, www.samhsa.gov/find-help/national-helpline.

38. Meah, Asad. "40 Inspirational John C. Maxwell Quotes On Success." *Awaken The Greatness Within*, November 16, 2016, https://www.awakenthegreatnesswithin.com/40-inspirational-john-c-maxwell-quotes-on-success/.

39. Jam. 2:26 (KJV)

40. 1 Cor. 13:2 (KJV)

41. Winfrey, Oprah. "The Powerful Lesson Maya Angelou Taught Oprah." *Oprah's Life Class* video, 4:16, posted by Oprah Winfrey Network, October 19, 2011, http://www.oprah.com/oprahs-lifeclass/the-powerful-lesson-maya-angelou-taught-oprah-video.

REFERENCES

Backe, Caleb. "Frankincense Essential Oil Benefits: Frankly, It's Fantastic." *Maple Holistics*, 29 Oct. 2019, www.mapleholistics.com/blog/frankincense-essential-oil-benefits/.

Buckler's Team. "The Many (So Many!) Benefits of Sweet Almond Oil for Your Skin." *Buckler's*, 23 Jan. 2017, https://bucklersremedy.com/blogs/the-dirty/the-many-so-many-benefits-of-sweet-almond-oil-for-your-skin.

Fletcher, Jenna. "10 Best Essential Oils for Wrinkles: What Works Best and Why?" *Medical News Today*, 27 Apr. 2018, www.medicalnewstoday.com/articles/321645.php.

Granero, Kristin, and Marissa Miller. "Olive Oil Can Literally Work Wonders on Your Hair." *Women's Health*, 9 Mar. 2019, www.womenshealthmag.com/beauty/g19897047/beauty-benefits-of-olive-oil/.

McCulloch, Marsha. "14 Benefits and Uses of Rosemary Essential Oil." *Healthline*, 15 Nov. 2108, www.healthline.com/nutrition/rosemary-oil-benefits.

Micah. "25 Healing Benefits of Peppermint Oil." *Alyaka: The Art of Beauty*, 14 June 2017, www.alyaka.com/magazine/25-healing-benefits-peppermint-oil/.

Perkins, Sabrina. "How to Soothe Your Irritated Scalp with This Natural Oil." *Naturally Curly*, 23 Mar. 2015, www.naturallycurly.com/curlreading/home/how-to-soothe-your-irritated-scalp-with-this-natural-oil.

Rajapet, Meenal. "10 Benefits of Mint (Pudina) For Skin And 11 Ways to Use It." *Stylecraze*, 26 Sept. 2019, www.stylecraze.com/articles/10-skin-benefits-of-mint/.

Spritzler, Franziska. "14 Everyday Uses for Tea Tree Oil." *Healthline*, 21 Apr. 2017, www.healthline.com/nutrition/tea-tree-oil.

TNN. "Here's How Cranberries Can Work Wonders for Your Skin and Hair! - Times of India." *The Times of India*, 12 Feb. 2019, timesofindia.indiatimes.com/life-style/food-news/heres-how-cranberries-can-work-wonders-for-your-skin-and-hair/articleshow/67945103.cms.

Villines, Zawn. "10 Benefits of Vitamin E Oil." *Medical News Today*, 30 June 2017, www.medicalnewstoday.com/articles/318168.php.

Watson, Kathryn. "Egg Yolk for Hair." Edited by Cynthia Cobb, *Healthline*, 18 Dec. 2017, www.healthline.com/health/egg-yolk-for-hair.

Wong, Cathy. "How Castor Oil Can Help Moisturize Your Scalp and Hair." *Verywell Health*, 2 July 2019, www.verywellhealth.com/using-castor-oil-for-hair-growth-4172190.

Wyman, Christine. "Mayo in Hair – Does It Work? How to Use?" *Wild About Beauty*, 27 Sept. 2019, wildaboutbeauty.com/mayo-in-hair/.

JOURNAL

#100WaysToLoveYourself #BelieveBecomeRepeat

#100WaysToLoveYourself #BelieveBecomeRepeat

#100WaysToLoveYourself #BelieveBecomeRepeat

#100WaysToLoveYourself #BelieveBecomeRepeat

#100WaysToLoveYourself #BelieveBecomeRepeat

#100WaysToLoveYourself #BelieveBecomeRepeat

#100WaysToLoveYourself #BelieveBecomeRepeat

#100WaysToLoveYourself #BelieveBecomeRepeat

#100WaysToLoveYourself #BelieveBecomeRepeat

#100WaysToLoveYourself #BelieveBecomeRepeat

#100WaysToLoveYourself #BelieveBecomeRepeat

#100WaysToLoveYourself #BelieveBecomeRepeat

_____

_____

_____

_____

_____

_____

_____

_____

_____

_____

_____

_____

_____

_____

_____

_____

_____

_____

_____

_____

_____

_____

#100WaysToLoveYourself #BelieveBecomeRepeat

#100WaysToLoveYourself #BelieveBecomeRepeat

#100WaysToLoveYourself #BelieveBecomeRepeat

#100WaysToLoveYourself #BelieveBecomeRepeat

Made in the USA
Las Vegas, NV
03 April 2022

46792809R10111